THE WORLD FOLKTALE LIBRARY

Tales from China

By Annie Bergeret and Marie Tenaille

Illustrated by Françoise Boudignon

SILVER BURDETT COMPANY

Morristown, New Jersey
Glenview, Ill. • Palo Alto • Dallas • Altanta

© Librairie Hachette, 1977. Adapted and published in the United States by Silver Burdett Company, Morristown, N. J. 1981 Printing.

Library of Congress Catalog Card No. 80-52513   ISBN 0-382-06596-4

CONTENTS

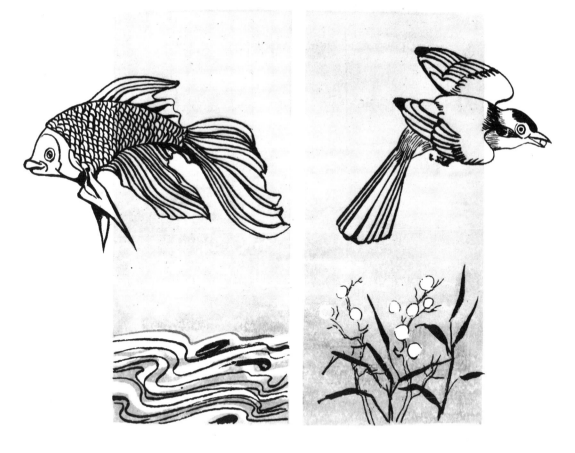

The Magic Brush of Ma Liang

Ma Liang was much too poor to go to school, but ever since he learned how to hold a little stick in his hand, Ma Liang drew! He could draw everything he saw — birds, fish, flowers, trees — anything at all.

Ma Liang had only one dream — to own a real brush to paint with. But Ma Liang was quite happy while he was waiting for his dream to come true. He could draw with his little stick on the sand, with his wet fingers on the rocks at the edge of the river, or with a piece of charcoal on the walls of his little house. The birds he drew were so lifelike that you expected to hear them sing, and his fish so well done that you believed you were seeing them swim.

Suddenly one night, Ma Liang saw standing before him an old man with a white beard and a long purple tunic. Ma Liang had never seen this man before, but he was not afraid. The old man seemed pleasant and friendly and Ma Liang watched him with astonishment.

The old man did not say a word, but Ma Liang saw that he was holding a brush out to him. Ma Liang's heart jumped for joy, but he did not dare put out his hand to take this brush. It seemed much too beautiful for him. The handle of the brush was made of solid gold and its white bristles shone like silver!

However, he heard the old man say to him, "Take this brush, Ma Liang. It is yours! Remember that you must always use it for good, and you must never give it to anyone!"

Then Ma Liang's joy was boundless. He gazed at the magnificent brush he had just received and he jumped with delight!

"Thank you, grandfather! Thank you!" he said.

But the old man had disappeared and Ma Liang woke up on his mat. Was it only a dream? And yet, in his right hand Ma Liang held very tightly an extraordinary brush, the brush of his dream, a brush of solid gold!

At daybreak Ma Liang wet his brush, dipped it in ink, and painted a bird. The painted bird shook its wings, looked at the child, and flew out of Ma Liang's open window into the sky, singing joyously!

Dumbfounded, Ma Liang realized that the brush he had received while dreaming was magic! Next he painted a fish. The fish shook its tail, moved its fins, looked at Ma Liang, and slid off the edge of the window, into the brook, then into the river. Ma Liang, filled with delight, saw it make a thousand turns in the water and head towards the sea.

Yes, his brush was truly magic, and Ma Liang promised himself to use it to do good, as the sage had instructed, and not to entrust it to anyone!

One morning, instead of going to gather firewood as he did every other morning, little Ma Liang put his brush under his tunic, took a roll of paper under his arm, attached an inkwell

to his belt, and started to walk through the village. Since his drawings could become real, he was going to have a lot to do!

As soon as they understood that the golden brush of Ma Liang was magic, the villagers ran up to him. Each one had something to ask of him.

The boy drew a hoe for the man who had broken his, a plough for the one who had none, a lamp for the man who needed one, a pail for the one who had lost his! The villagers were astounded and delighted and from that day on, Ma Liang and his brush spread joy wherever they went.

Lord Tsaï was a rich and envious noble whose land bordered on Ma Liang's village. Lord Tsaï had heard a great deal about the child and his golden brush and he wanted them for himself. So he ordered his servants to seize Ma Liang and bring the young artist back to him at once.

As soon as Ma Liang was brought before him, Tsaï gave him an enormous roll of paper and some marvelous inks. Then he asked Ma Liang to paint fabulous jewels and rich fabrics for his treasure chests, fleet horses for his stables, and arms for his guards.

Fortunately, little Ma Liang had not forgotten the words of the old man. He judged that it was not wise to obey Lord Tsaï, who already had countless riches and whose heart was as hard as stone. Ma Liang refused to make a single drawing for him.

Furious, Lord Tsaï took back the great roll of paper and wonderful inks. Then he had Ma Liang imprisoned in an empty stable at the end of his garden. He forbade his servants to bring him anything to eat or drink. Lord Tsaï abandoned Ma Liang there for three days, convinced that the solitude, hunger, and thirst would soon make him change his mind.

But Ma Liang had kept his brush under his tunic, and he still had his little roll of paper and his own inkwell. So he was able to paint all the things that he needed — a table to draw on, some good food, a mat to sleep on, and a stove to warm the stable and cook his food.

On the morning of the third day, Lord Tsaï opened his window and noticed that a thick blanket of snow covered his courtyard and gardens. Suddenly he remembered Ma Liang whom he had ordered to be imprisoned in an empty and freezing stable. He thought that perhaps Ma Liang had died of cold during the night, if he was not already dead from hunger!

Without saying anything to his servants, Lord Tsaï decided to go to the stable himself. As he approached, he saw a warm light shining under the door. A delicious odor of black mushroom soup awakened his appetite! He looked through the keyhole and to his great astonishment saw Ma Liang seated at a table with a bowl of soup in front of him, devouring some crusty sesame seed cakes, while in a stove a roaring red hot fire warmed the room!

"Which one of you dared treat Ma Liang like a prince?" he asked of all his servants. "This boy has refused to obey me; he must be punished!"

Lord Tsaï was obliged however to consider the evidence. Ma Liang had painted all these things with his magic paint brush!

Furious, Tsaï ordered his servants to seize the brush and to kill Ma Liang. But in his anger he shouted so loudly that Ma Liang heard him. The boy immediately drew a ladder that came up to the stable window. He escaped down the ladder and disappeared into the countryside.

When the servants of Lord Tsaï went into the stable, Ma Liang was no longer there. All of the objects that had enabled Ma Liang to survive had also disappeared! Lord Tsaï, noticing the ladder against the wall, climbed up the first rungs, but then he fell heavily to the ground. The magic ladder had disappeared!

Ma Liang did not set forth towards his native village. He thought it would be wiser not to return there, for the furious Lord Tsaï would be able to find him easily, even if he hid among friends. Ma Liang felt very sad at having to leave his home and go far away, but he promised himself that he would return someday. Then with his magic brush, he painted a beautiful black horse, mounted it, and rode off at a gallop.

He was still galloping when shouts and the noise of many horsemen made him turn around. Alas for Ma Liang! Lord Tsaï and his armed guards were coming after him, pursuing him angrily!

Little Ma Liang was very frightened. He did not wish to die because of his magic brush, but at the same time, he refused to surrender it into the hands of Lord Tsaï. Ma Liang reined in his horse, took his brush from under his tunic, and drew a bow and arrow.

The pursuers were now very close. Tsaï was at their head, shouting and brandishing his shining sword.

"Ma Liang! If you value your life, give me your brush!"

And Ma Liang answered, "Lord Tsaï, give up your pursuit or you will perish! This brush has been entrusted to me, it cannot belong to you!"

Ma Liang waited until the last moment to draw his bow, and——PFFT——his arrow flew straight into the neck of Lord Tsaï, who rolled to the ground.

The boy spurred his mount and the horse sped away at a triple gallop. He traveled thus on horseback for three days and three nights and finally stopped in the little village of Yan-Lan where no one knew him. There at last he felt he was safe.

Then Ma Liang decided that he would earn his living from his paintings. He would sell them in the street. However, always fearful that his pictures would come to life and again call attention to him, he also decided that he would leave his pictures unfinished. It was indeed a good idea!

"I'll manage," he said to himself, "to forget a beak, an eye, or a wing on my birds; and if my fishes are missing a fin, the villagers will not even notice it! They will not be able to discover that my brush is magic. My drawings will not come to life if they are not finished."

So Ma Liang lived many moons, painting and selling his pictures every day. But it happened one day that just as he was painting a white crane, a drop of Chinese ink fell accidentally on the spot where the eye that Ma Liang wanted to leave out should be. Now the painting of the bird was complete!

To the astonishment of the villagers of Yan-Lan, the bird opened his eye, fluttered his wings, uttered a cry, and flew away!

Immediately the people began to talk of the marvelous painter with a magic brush. The news soon reached the ears of the emperor, who wished to see the young painter.

Ma Liang had not forgotten his recent adventures. He preferred not to show his talents and his brush to the emperor, who he knew was cruel and unjust. But the more Ma Liang was in demand the more the emperor wanted to see the young painter, for he too wanted to make use of the magic brush.

And before Ma Liang had time to run away, the soldiers of the emperor seized him and dragged him to the imperial palace.

"Ma Liang," the emperor said to him, "I have heard about your marvelous talent. Is it true that your brush gives life to everything you paint?"

"It is true that has happened, Your Majesty," answered Ma Liang, who did not dare lie to the emperor, "but I can only use my brush to do good and I cannot entrust it to anyone!"

"That should not prevent you from painting a dragon for the emperor!" cried the emperor already angry.

Ma Liang forthwith took out his brush, and pretending not to be able to paint a dragon, painted instead a horrible toad, which started to croak and hop around the emperor.

The emperor, disgusted by this beast, ordered Ma Liang to draw him a phoenix at once if he wanted to live. However instead of painting the fabulous bird, Ma Liang imprudently drew a defeathered rooster, which began to soil the magnificent draperies that covered the throne of the emperor.

Now the anger of the emperor was terrible! He ordered his soldiers to seize the golden brush from Ma Liang and to shut the boy up in the tower.

With the magic brush in his hand, the emperor secluded himself in his study and began to paint a great pile of gold. Because he was a greedy man and never had enough, and since it seemed so easy with the magic brush, he painted a second pile of gold, then a third, then a fourth! The emperor saw all this gold and could not stop, and the brush went on and on painting gold.

Yet when he lifted his head from his work, he noticed that his study was filled, not by countless mounds of gold as he thought, but by enormous piles of stones so badly piled up that the largest, placed on top, began to tumble down threatening to crush him!

"Help! Help!" cried the emperor, clapping his hands for his servants to come to him. "This brush is bewitched by Ma Liang! Go get him out of his prison and bring him to me!"

While the guards went to get Ma Liang from the tower, the emperor could not resist making one more try. Since he still wanted gold, he would paint a golden brick. He would paint just one brick, but he would make it enormous—several meters long!

When the painting was finished, the emperor found that instead of seeing a golden brick before him, there was a terrible snake that lurched toward him with wide open jaws. The huge snake would have swallowed him whole, if his ministers had not rushed to his aid.

At this moment, Ma Liang entered surrounded by the emperor's guards. The monarch, frightened by what had just happened, understood at last that the magic brush would never obey him, but would always turn against him. He pleaded with Ma Liang to forgive him for having him imprisoned.

"I will return your magic brush to you, Ma Liang! I promise you! But first, tell me you will paint everything I ask you to!"

Ma Liang was not stupid and he had a plan. So he pretended to accept, for he absolutely had to have his brush back.

"Return my brush to me, Majesty, and I will paint all that you desire. Do you wish a forest around your palace? Or the sea and all its fish?"

Happy to see the boy so submissive, the emperor immediately gave him the brush. Then he started to think about what he was going to ask of him.

"If I ask him to paint me a forest," he said to himself, "he'll put ferocious beasts in it and I will be devoured! I am not going to ask him again for a dragon or a phoenix or an extraordinary animal or piles of gold. I have seen where that can lead! It would be better if he painted the sea for me—the blue sea to encircle my palace!"

With three strokes of the brush, the sea was there in front of the emperor; his ministers and guards were astonished. The blue sea shone all around his palace, which was now an island! It was an immense and transparent sea, without a ripple, brilliant and smooth as a mirror. However, this still was not enough for the emperor.

"Why are there not any fish in this sea?" he asked severely.

Ma Liang made several little strokes with his brush here and there, and the sea was immediately filled with fish of all sizes and colors. They frolicked about joyously; they seemed so happy as they played. But when they saw the mean, cruel, and greedy face of the emperor bending over them, they all swam away toward the open sea. The emperor, furious at seeing them disappear, rushed up to Ma Liang and ordered him, "Quick! A ship! Make me a ship! I want to go out to sea to find my fish!"

Ma Liang did not have to be urged, he immediately began to paint a huge Chinese vessel while the emperor became more and more impatient.

"Hurry, Ma Liang! I want to go to sea with my entire company!"

As soon as the ship was finished, the emperor embarked with his ministers and his guards. But the ship remained motionless because there wasn't the slightest breath of wind.

"Make us some wind! Make us some wind, Ma Liang!" shouted the emperor, wavings his arms on the bridge.

Ma Liang, with several strokes of his magic brush, made a breeze arise. The surface of the sea rippled and the vessel sailed lightly out to sea.

But the emperor felt that the ship was not moving fast enough. From the bridge of the ship he began to shout again, "A little more wind, you lazy one, a little more wind!"

Ma Liang obeyed. With the large strokes of his brush on his picture, the waves rose and the sails swelled in the rushing wind. The vessel pitched and started to head straight for the open sea at tremendous speed.

On the bridge of the ship, the emperor was shouting himself hoarse, "Stop, Ma Liang! Stop! There is enough wind now!"

But Ma Liang's brush would no longer stop. It was not able to stop! It continued to make huge curves on the sea and large thunderbolts in the sky. The sea became turbulent, the wind became violent. Enormous waves rolled onto the bridge of the ship. The wind ripped the sails and tore up the masts!

The emperor cried out to Ma Liang, begging him to stop the tempest. Ma Liang, who knew just how far the cruelty and greediness of the emperor could go, did not listen to him. He continued to paint a magnificent storm.

The sky became black. Night began to fall. The furious waves continued to beat like immense walls of water against the ship, which finally sank with the entire crew and all its treasures. The emperor, his ministers, and his guards went to meet the fish!

Ma Liang returned alone to the palace, for he wished to get his horse and return to his native village.

After the death of the emperor, no one ever again tried to steal Ma Liang's magic brush, which became more and more famous throughout all of China. Ma Liang could finally use it for everything that seemed good to him, spending his time painting for the poor people.

However, one might sometimes look for Ma Liang and not find him. For while he was often in his village, he also traveled throughout the countryside, painting for those who truly needed him.

Old Wang-Niang and
Her Silver Coin

Old Wang-Niang had lived alone for a very long time and, in her solitude, often talked with the objects in her house—the rice pot, the grindstone, the water jug, and the spinning wheel.

One beautiful morning, while sweeping the earthen floor of her house, the old lady found a brand new Chinese silver coin! Poor Wang-Niang had not often seen such a coin, and as no one had come into her house, she concluded that the coin had just appeared by itself and that it belonged to her.

"Guard my silver coin!" she said to her rice pot. She put the coin in the bottom of the pot and carefully closed it with the lid.

As for the rice — the old woman didn't have very much of it left. She had eaten some for her lunch and had left just a handful for her supper. There was hardly enough to cover her beautiful silver coin.

But that evening at suppertime, she noticed that her pot had somehow become almost half full during the day. Old Wang-Niang was delighted to be able to eat as much rice as she wished for her supper. She again left just a handful of rice in the pot for her meal the next day, hardly enough to cover her beautiful silver coin.

And the next morning she noticed that her pot was again half filled with rice! In her joy, the old woman opened her door to let in the sun, and began to sing:

> In my rice pot
> A silver coin I have placed.
>
> I have rice.
> Some good rice.
>
> My silver coin
> Gives me white rice.
>
> I have rice.
> Some good rice.
>
> A magic silver coin
> In my pot of rice!

Her neighbors heard her sing and rejoiced with her, but the tiger of the mountain, who prowled not far from there, also heard it. Without ceremony, he came to ask old Wang-Niang to give him her silver coin.

"No!" answered the old woman. "You shall not have it, even if you come to ask me for it ten times!"

"WRAOUOUOUH!" loudly roared the furious tiger. "I will have it anyway, and no later than this evening, when I will have eaten you, you old carcass!"

Poor frightened Wang-Niang started to cry, first at the idea of ending her days in the teeth of the tiger, but also because she was going to lose her silver coin. Then she pulled herself together and decided to resist. She knew very well how to defend herself against the villainous tiger!

She got up and started to sharpen her sickle.

"Zzzz! Zzzz!" went the sharpening stone, and "Sharp! Sharp!" answered the sickle.

Upon hearing these noises, the dried peas on the table asked the old woman, "Grandmother Wang-Niang, there is nothing to mow outside, why are you sharpening your sickle so hard?"

"The tiger of the mountain is going to come tonight to take my silver coin from me, but I will cut off his head first!" answered the woman.

"We will help you, grandmother," said the peas. "We will roll on the ground, you will see!" And they let themselves roll down in front of the door.

"Zzzz! Zzzz!" still went the sharpening stone, and "Sharp! Sharp!" answered the sickle.

On hearing these sounds the egg that was in the cupboard asked the old woman, "Grandmother Wang-Niang, there is nothing to mow outside, why are you sharpening your sickle so hard?"

"The tiger of the mountain wants to take my silver coin, but I will cut off his head first!"

"I will help you, grandmother. I will sit on the hearth, you will see!" And the egg went to sit in the fireplace.

"Zzzz! Zzzz!" the sharpening stone kept saying, and "Sharp! Sharp!" always answered the sickle, which was not yet sharp enough.

At the noise, the little crab came out of its hole and asked,

"Grandmother Wang-Niang, there is nothing to mow outside, why are you sharpening your sickle so hard?"

"The tiger of the mountain wants my silver coin. He will come tonight to eat me. But I will cut off his head first!"

"Well, I'll help you, grandmother. I'll wait in the water jug, you will see!" And the little crab hopped up to the jug and climbed in.

"Zzzz! Zzzz!" continued the sharpening stone and "Sharp! Sharp!" answered the sickle, which became sharper and sharper.

At this noise, the big, thick stick standing near the fireplace asked, "Grandmother Wang-Niang, there is nothing to mow outside, why do you sharpen your sickle so hard?"

"The tiger of the mountain wants to come to eat me and steal my silver coin hidden in the bottom of my rice pot! But I am not going to let him!"

"Very well, I will help you grandmother. I will place myself at the edge of your bed, and I will defend you!" And the big stick climbed up on the edge of the bed.

"Zzzz! Zzzz!" continued the sharpening stone, and "Sharp! Sharp!" answered the sickle, which had become as sharp as a sword.

At this noise, the frog came out of her hole, took a big jump, and asked, "Grandmother Wang-Niang, there is nothing to mow outside, why do you sharpen your sickle so hard?"

"It's for the tiger of the mountain! I expect him tonight; he is supposed to come to eat me and steal my piece of silver!"

"Don't worry, grandmother. I will be there near the head of your bed!" And the frog jumped up to the head of the bed where she crouched waiting.

"Zzzz! Zzzz!" the sharpening stone kept going, and "Sharp! Sharp!" always answered the sickle, whose blade shone like a saber!

At the noise, the spinning wheel sitting in its place asked, "Grandmother Wang-Niang, there is nothing to mow outside, why do you sharpen your sickle so hard?"

"It's to cut off the head of the tiger of the mountain! He is coming to eat me tonight and steal my silver coin!"

"Do not worry, grandmother. I will be there in the corner of the room, and he'll hear me!" And the spinning wheel went to stand in the corner.

"Zzzz! Zzzz!" the sharpening stone went on, and "Sharp! Sharp!" always answered the sickle, which sparkled like a brand new one and cut like a sword.

At the noise, the hammer, which was on the shelf said, "Grandmother Wang-Niang, there is nothing to mow outdoors. Stop sharpening your sickle! It is time to sleep."

"But night is falling, and the tiger of the mountain is coming down to eat me and steal my silver coin!"

"He will not take it from you" exclaimed the hammer, jumping about in fury, and—boom—it went to put itself on the doorframe. "Count on me, he will not eat you!" he said again.

When night had fallen, the old woman went to bed just as she did every evening, but tonight she placed her well-sharpened sickle alongside her.

A little later, the tiger of the mountain came as he said he would. Old Wang-Niang heard him approaching.

With a shove of his head, the tiger lunged at the door, which opened wide. But, hardly had he entered the room when the peas, which were waiting in front of the door, began to roll in all directions, and—kerplop—the tiger slipped and landed with his four paws in the air!

He got up and groped for the live coals from the fireplace. He put his snout near the fire and began to blow and blow on the fire to fan the flames and make more light.

But the egg was there, hidden under the ashes and—pouff—it burst in his face! His eyes were filled with ashes and he couldn't see a thing.

With a great deal of difficulty the tiger found the water jug so that he might wash the ashes out of his eyes. He plunged his right paw in to take up some water, but the crab, who was waiting in the jug, caught his paw and bit it!

"WAOUOUOUH!" The tiger roared with pain and quickly withdrew his paw. With one leap he headed towards the bed of the old woman.

But the big, thick stick, which was on the edge of the bed, got up and—bong—dealt him a good strong blow on his skull. In one instant the tiger of the mountain thought he saw all the stars of the night.

At the head of the bed, the frog, which was at its post, began to croak, "Rrribit! Rrribit! Hit him harder, harder!"

And the spinning wheel, waiting in the corner, did not forget its promise and began to spin all by itself while saying "Ron-ron. We've got him! We've got him!"

Then the tiger—tripped by the peas, blinded by the ashes, bitten by the crab, beaten by the stick, stunned by the frog, and frightened by the spinning wheel—started to make his retreat even before old Grandmother Wang-Niang had time to get up, brandishing her well-sharpened sickle.

The tiger of the mountain charged for the door, but he slipped again on the peas, which danced around on the floor under his feet, and he fell against the door. At this moment, the hammer, which was waiting there, fell — boom — on his head with a dull thud.

The animal forgot the silver coin and old Wang-Niang! He no longer thought of anything but to escape to his mountain. And he never again came near the house of the old woman, who always kept her silver coin safe at the bottom of the pot. And the pot was always half filled with rice.

The Wind Pearl

Centuries and centuries ago in the region of Yu Shu there was a kingdom called Poula. Its territory stretched between the mountains into a vast plain where great herds of sheep and cattle grazed. The population was large and happy, but the people could only feed themselves by raising and caring for their animals, for no grain—neither corn, nor barley, nor sorghum, nor wheat—grew in this faraway kingdom. Not a single grain of cereal had ever been seen there!

However the soil was fertile, and in the garden of the king of Poula grew marvelous fruit trees and delightful lotus blossoms.

The only son of the king, young Prince Ha Xin, was already known for his intelligence, his courage, and his endurance. Ha Xin often listened to the pilgrims and travelers who passed through Poula. Thus he learned that in the kingdom of the God of the Mountain, called the Land of Yiouta, there were plants that grew tall and formed healthy seeds. These seeds, once planted, produced excellent grain with a good taste, which could be ground, kneaded, and cooked for food.

Ha Xin wished that all the people of Poula could be nourished by this good grain. He decided to go himself to the country of the God of the Mountain. He would ask him for some seeds from these wonderful plants to bring back to his kingdom.

On his sixteenth birthday, Ha Xin told his parents, the king and queen of Poula, about his plan. But his parents knew that in order to get to Yiouta, it would be necessary to travel more than nine thousand li, which was a very great distance and meant months and months of journeying. Their son would also have to climb ninety-nine mountains and cross as many rivers!

"You are our only son," they said to Prince Ha Xin. "We fear that you will encounter too many great dangers on your way, insurmountable dangers! We beg of you to give up this perilous voyage."

But the prince would not listen to them. He was so resolved to carry out his plan that the king and queen were obliged to consent. Since they certainly did not intend to let the prince leave alone for such a dangerous expedition, they armed twenty of their best warriors with lance and saber and gave them the mission of accompanying Ha Xin into the Land of Yiouta.

However, in the course of scaling so many mountains, of crossing so many wide rivers and immense forests, of traveling through so many different kingdoms, all of Prince Ha Xin's men died, one after the other. Some were killed by enemy warriors, others by highwaymen, others were bitten by venomous snakes or devoured by tigers. Those who remained died of exhaustion or discouragement.

After climbing the ninety-eighth mountain and crossing the ninety-eighth river, only Prince Ha Xin and his horse remained alive.

The sides of the last mountain were so steep, that the prince had to get off his horse and climb on foot while holding the animal by the bridle. When he arrived at the top, he saw that the sun was shining like fire there, and he was very surprised to discover an old woman seated under a large pine tree, busily spinning.

Ha Xin, happy to meet someone at last, greeted her politely and asked her the way to the Land of Yiouta. At first the old lady looked at him from head to toe without saying a word. Then the prince explained to her who he was, where he came from, and why it was necessary for him to see the God of the Mountain.

The woman then said to him, "You wish to see Yiouta, Prince Ha Xin! That will be easy for you, now that you have come this far. When you get to the foot of this mountain you will see a river flowing. Follow the river all the way to its source. You will soon come to a magnificent waterfall. Stop there and call out the name of Yiouta three times. He will come!"

Even before Prince Ha Xin had time to thank the old woman, she had disappeared.

The prince of the Kingdom of Poula started out again. He descended the ninety-ninth mountain, crossed the ninety-ninth river, followed the river upstream, and suddenly found himself in front of a great waterfall that fell with a tremendous roar from the top of the mountain.

Ha Xin stood directly in front of the waterfall and saluted respectfully. With a strong voice he called the God of the Mountain and said to him, "Honorable Yiouta, would you please be so kind as to show yourself, I have something to ask you."

Hardly had Ha Xin finished calling the god, when an old

man as big as a mountain came out of the waterfall. His beard, white as snow, fell from the top of the mountain down to the river. Ha Xin found himself face to face with the God Yiouta!

"Who is calling me?" asked the giant, lowering his head to see who was at his feet.

"Great God of the Mountain! It is I, Ha Xin, the prince of the faraway Kingdom of Poula," began the young man.

"And what do you wish?" asked the god.

"I have come to you because I heard that you have much fine grain here. I would like to ask you for some seeds to take back with me to plant in my country so our people might have good, nourishing grain to eat."

"What? Grain from here?" said King Yiouta in a loud voice. Then he burst into a great laugh that shook the whole mountain. Its enormous echo resounded a long time, while the waterfall stopped falling.

"But my little prince, you have been fooled! It is only in the country of Kepoulah, the King of the Serpents, where there are plantations of grain."

Prince Ha Xin was very disappointed and remained silent for a moment. Then he asked, "Can you tell me where the King of Serpents lives and if he will wish to give me some seeds?"

Yiouta answered him smiling, "With a good horse like yours, in seven days and seven nights you will be there. But Kepoulah is a cruel king, stingy and mean, he will never agree to give you seeds with which to feed your people, never! And do you know that all those who come to ask him for such seeds he changes into dogs in order to eat them? If you go there, you risk being changed into a dog and eaten yourself! Are you afraid, Ha Xin?"

"No!" said the young man. "I am not afraid and I want those seeds. But can you tell me, God of the Mountain, what I must do to obtain them?"

"In order to have these seeds, there is only one thing for you to do. You must steal some from the King of the Serpents! Since you are so persistent and courageous, I am going to tell you exactly how you must act.

"After the harvest, King Kepoulah puts the seeds into sacks, hides them under his throne, and has them guarded by his soldiers. But each day at the hour when the sun is at its highest, the king leaves his throne to go to the edge of the lake to meet the King of the Dragons. This takes only moments, barely the time necessary to burn a stick of incense. But his guards will take advantage of his absence to have a nap. It is exactly at that instant that you will have to get hold of the seeds."

When he finished speaking, seeing that Prince Ha Xin listened to him so attentively, the God of the Mountain took from inside his tunic a tiny little seed, no bigger than a grain of rice. Giving it to the young man, he said, "It is not possible for me to tell you more! But I give you this 'wind pearl' Prince Ha Xin. It will be able to help you in case of danger. When you are in trouble, remember to put it in your mouth. It will enable you to run as fast as the wind."

Ha Xin took the wind pearl and thanked Yiouta. The God of the Mountain gave him one last piece of advice.

"If, by misfortune, the King of the Serpents changes you into a dog, save yourself with your wind pearl. Run fast towards the east, always towards the east, until you meet a young girl with a pure heart who loves you. Then you will finally be able to return to your country where you will regain the form of a man! Go, Prince Ha Xin! The God of the Mountain wishes you good luck!"

When Ha Xin arrived in the land of the King of the Serpents, the harvests had already been taken in. He saw only the fields of thatch, which stretched as far as the eye could see.

The young man knew that King Kepoulah lived way on the top of the mountain, not far from the lake where the King of the Dragons lived. He got down from his horse, took the pouch that was on the horse's back, and hung it around his neck. Then he released the bridle of the steed and let the animal return alone to the Kingdom of Poula.

When he arrived at the top of the mountain, he chose a little cave that was exactly opposite the palace of Kepoulah. From there he could see everything that went on in the palace of the King of the Serpents.

At noon, just as Yiouta had told him, Ha Xin saw the King of the Serpents come out, accompanied by his bodyguards, and head for the lake. Kepoulah seemed enormous to him, fearsome and monstrous. He wore a kind of armor of green shells at the bottom of which hung a series of little silver bells that tinkled with each of his movements.

The moment had come for Ha Xin to enter into the palace of

the king and to reach the throne. He came out of his hiding place and crawled silently up to the door of the palace. He passed quickly in front of the two guards, who were already snoring. And at last Ha Xin entered the forbidding palace of the King of the Serpents!

The inside of the palace was dark and seemed more like a cave than a king's palace. Ha Xin walked through the halls, groping along the walls as he looked impatiently for the throne room. Finally, after many wrong turns, he came into a large room in the middle of which shone an enormous throne of gold mounted on a high platform and surrounded by lamps that were never supposed to go out.

In front of the platform, Ha Xin saw a row of sleeping guards and under the platform many sacks of grain were piled up.

It was the moment so long awaited by the young prince and his heart jumped for joy, however he kept calm and remained prudent. He wove in and out between the sleeping guards, slid up to the sacks of grain, and opened the nearest one. Handful by handful, without making the slighest noise, Ha Xin filled the pouch that was hanging around his neck.

He took a last handful, which he kept in his right hand, and skillfully made his way back to the guards. He found them still sound asleep and left the throne room without accident.

But the prince was so happy on leaving the palace, that he forgot the two guards who were sleeping at the entrance, and he had the misfortune to brush up against them a little in passing. Immediately, the two men awakened with a start, got up with a shout, and barred the passage with their lances.

Ha Xin threw the grain that he had in his hand into their faces, and while they rubbed their eyes, he drew out his saber and killed one of them. He was going to kill the second one, when the men in the throne room, awakened by the cries of the guards at the entrance, ran up and attacked him.

Prince Ha Xin was very courageous and he managed to kill

several of the armed guards. But then he knew that he must escape as fast as possible because he thought he heard the tinkling of the little bells announcing the return of the King of the Serpents.

However he was so excited and in such a rush, that he turned the wrong way and bumped violently into King Kepoulah, who was indeed coming back from the lake. Ha Xin was knocked down and surrounded on all sides. The guards ran up behind him and the king stood in front of him. Kepoulah's sneer froze the blood in Ha Xin's veins.

There was only one way out—the precipice on the east side of the palace. Ha Xin immediately put the wind pearl Yiouta had given him into his mouth and tried to run quickly toward the east side.

Suddenly there were three violent claps of thunder! It seemed to Ha Xin that lightning struck him several times, but he did not stop running. Before he could reach the precipice he realized that he had been transformed into a yellow dog! Fortunately the pouch filled with seeds was still hanging around his neck.

For an instant Ha Xin was bewildered. Then he remembered the advice of Yiouta, the God of the Mountain, and he dashed towards the east at a rush. And, thanks to the wind pearl which he still held in his mouth, it seemed he had wings. With a single leap, he crossed the precipice and flew over several high mountains. Behind him thunder echoed and lightning flashed because the anger of Kepoulah followed him but could not reach him.

Two years passed and still Ha Xin remained in the shape of a yellow dog. While following a large river, he had come to the country of Loujo. Cereal grains did not grow in this land either, but the earth was good and grass grew in abundance in the fields and on the surrounding mountains. Here the people lived in tribes and the chief of all the tribes was called Ken Pang. Ken Pang had three very beautiful daughters.

The third daughter, called Lan Fang, which means "Perfume of Orchids," was the most beautiful of the three and the one Ha Xin had preferred ever since the day of his arrival in Loujo. She seemed to be the most pleasant, the most intelligent, and surely the best of the three. She was a gentle girl and she loved plants, flowers, and animals. Remembering the words of Yiouta, Ha Xin thought that Lan Fang might be the young girl with the pure heart who could save him.

He decided to visit her and offer her his seeds of grain while waiting to be able to offer her his love. Lying in the field behind her father's house, he waited patiently for Lan Fang to come out to gather the flowers in the meadow as she often did. As soon as he saw her, he ran up to her. The young girl bent down to pet him and spoke to him softly.

Although his body had been changed into that of a yellow dog by the King of the Serpents, Ha Xin had kept his intelligent mind, and his glance expressed all his thoughts and sentiments. Lan Fang saw his look and understood that this yellow dog was not like other dogs. Then she opened the strange pouch that he was wearing at his neck and discovered with astonishment that it was filled with seeds of golden barley. Aided by the dog, who dug the earth with his paws, she planted several long rows of seeds.

From that moment on, Lan Fang and the yellow dog became inseparable friends. The young girl took him with her wherever she went. She loved this dog who had brought her the beautiful golden grain that remained a secret between them. Each day they went together to see their precious barley. They watched it sprout, grow, flower, and ripen.

It was now autumn and all the crops were ripe. One night when the moon was very full, Chief Ken Pang decided to arrange a gala dance on the lawn in front of his house to celebrate the good harvest. During this happy celebration, each one of his three young daughters would choose her future husband.

According to tradition, each girl was supposed to dance, carrying a basket of fruit in her arms. When she finished dancing, she was to offer the fruit to the one whom she would choose as a husband. Chief Ken Pang had invited the richest young men of the neighboring lands to the party, hoping, of course, that his daughters would choose them.

Luck seemed to smile on him. After the first dance and the second dance, at the sound of the flutes and the tambourines, his eldest daughter and his second daughter made their choices—choices that gladdened the heart of their father.

But then Lan Fang's turn came, she who was the most beautiful of all. She danced three times with gentle grace, but without finding the one whom she could love. As she looked at each one of the suitors, it seemed to her that they lacked

31

something, and not one had the good fortune to be chosen by her.

However, all the young men who were there greatly desired to win the hand of the lovely Lan Fang and they were very disappointed. When she danced a fourth time to obey her father, who seemed to boil with anger, she heard the annoyed young men murmur, "But what kind of a man does she want then? Doesn't she seem to prefer her dog to all of us?"

Filled with emotion on hearing this, Lan Fang let her basket of fruit fall on Ha Xin, who looked at her tenderly. Her family and all the guests overwhelmed her with ridicule, for according to the belief of the country, this was a dishonorable incident.

Her father arose and said to her angrily, "My daughter, since you have shown in front of everyone that you love this dog more than any young man, you have therefore chosen it in place of a husband! Leave with it and never again return to Loujo!"

Lan Fang's heart was broken, tears flowed down her cheeks like a cascade of pearls. Followed by the yellow dog, she headed for their barley field. The clusters of grain were ripe and bending toward them. They seemed to wish them good luck, but they could not console Lan Fang, who continued to weep.

"Lan Fang, do not cry any more!" said the yellow dog, who spoke aloud to his beloved for the first time.

Astonished, the young girl stopped sobbing and looked at Ha Xin in amazement.

"Do not be afraid, Lan Fang! Know that you are right to love me. I am a man and not a dog!"

Frightened, Lan Fang remained speechless for a long moment, and then she asked, "But if you are a man, why do you have the body of a dog?"

"Have you ever heard of the faraway Kingdom of Poula?" asked Ha Xin. "You must believe me when I tell you that I am the prince of that country and that I left my own land to look for barley seeds. My name is Ha Xin."

Then Ha Xin told Lan Fang how the King of the Serpents had changed him into a dog.

"But when will you be able to change back into a man," Lan Fang asked him, her face beaming, "so that the two of us can live happily together?"

"When I meet a young girl who loves me with a pure and sincere love, the God Yiouta assured me," answered Ha Xin.

"But I love you, Ha Xin. I love you with a love pure and sincere! Why have you not yet turned back into a man?" Lan Fang asked.

"If you truly love me," answered the prince, "you must quickly harvest all this barley. Then make a little pouch and fill it with barley seeds. Hang the pouch around my neck. Then I will go ahead of you, walking towards the Kingdom of Poula, and all along the way I will plant barley seeds. Follow me, going exactly in my footsteps, there where the barley will soon begin to grow. When you no longer see the barley growing, you will know that I am very near and that I await you impatiently."

Lan Fang did not say a word. Instead she began to reap the barley. When she had gathered in all the grain, she tore off a piece of her tunic and made of it a little pouch, which she filled with barley seeds. Then she hung the pouch around the neck of the yellow dog. She wanted to leave with him, but Ha Xin said she must not.

"If you love me, follow the route along which I am going to plant the barley seeds. You must no longer see me in this ugly form!"

Before Lan Fang had time to hold the yellow dog in her arms as she had often done before, Ha Xin had disappeared and begun his return journey to the Kingdom of Poula.

There was no real road and so Ha Xin walked in the open fields, stopping at almost every step to scratch the ground and put in some seeds.

Quite far behind, Lan Fang also walked. At the beginning, the seeds guided her on the route to Poula towards her beloved, but later it was the first sprouts that showed her the way. And as she slowly advanced, she saw the stems grow, and later she found the clusters of barley.

Lan Fang longed to catch up with Ha Xin. She wanted to run to see him again, to speak to him, to listen to him, but she knew that she must not. She continued to follow him as he had told her to do.

How long were they on the road, the two of them, eating the wild fruits, which they may have gathered from the same bushes, and drinking water from the same streams? Lan Fang could not tell, but she saw that autumn had come at last. She walked on until the moment the barley ripened and the leaves of the trees turned yellow.

Then she noticed a beautiful town in the distance. She had

endured many miseries, braved the rain, the wind, the frost, and the snow. But now her heart was full of joy. It was warm with love and happiness for now she knew she would soon arrive in the country of her beloved!

So Lan Fang entered the Kingdom of Poula. Her shoes were worn out, her clothes were in shreds, but her beauty shone as always, and her heart remained pure.

Hardly had she entered the town, when she noticed that there were no longer any barley plants to guide her, but instead she saw beautiful trees and flowers, and lovely houses. Each time she met someone she asked, "Have you seen a yellow dog?"

Finally a woman answered her, "Yes, I met him and I saw him pass through the gates of the palace this morning!"

Lan Fang now had only to follow the main road of Poula which led to the palace. She saw the palace from afar, surrounded by flowers and trees. It was a magnificent castle, a fit home for her beloved Ha Xin!

When Lan Fang entered the park of the King of Poula, she noticed the yellow dog coming toward her. But at the same time she became dazed. It seemed to her that the dog disappeared in a cloud. When the cloud vanished, Prince Ha Xin appeared to her for the first time, and Lan Fang fell into his arms.

They had finally found each other again after a long and difficult trial. And each was as young and as beautiful as before!

Prince Ha Xin presented Lan Fang to his parents, who shed tears of joy on regaining their son. They had thought they would never see him again, since his horse had returned without him. And they immediately loved beautiful Lan Fang, with her complexion like ivory and rose and her long hair like ebony.

Lan Fang married Ha Xin that very evening. It was a magnificent wedding attended by the entire population of the Kingdom of Poula. The people celebrated the courage of the prince, who had gone so far to look for the barley seeds. And they praised the fidelity of Lan Fang, who had followed the barley seeds for thousands of li to find her prince.

The barley was already growing in all the regions that they had crossed, and everywhere the people rejoiced. And Prince Ha Xin and Princess Lan Fang lived a long and happy life in the Kingdom of Poula.

The Monster of the Forest
of Tian

One day a peculiar and unknown animal arrived in the forest of Tian. From the top of his camphor tree, the monkey was the first to see it and hear it cry out. Terrified, the monkey fled without taking the time to observe the strange animal. Hop, hop—the monkey jumped from branch to branch to go warn the fox.

"There is a monster! I saw a monster in our forest! He has the head of a horse, but he has long ears and he is covered with long hair. When he cries out, he makes a frightful, deafening noise, enough to make all the creatures of the forest flee!"

The fox hurried to go see for himself. He slipped in between the trunks of the trees and, without a sound, approached the strange animal.

"He doesn't look so terrible!" he said to himself. "Let's wait and see."

But when the monster started to bray, the fox took flight and ran straight to the tiger to tell him what he had just discovered.

"I've seen a monster that eats grass and makes the most horrible noises!"

"Let's go see who this intruder is and what he can do," said the tiger. And he asked the fox to take him to the monster.

All this time the monster, who did not suspect a thing and was very comfortable in this forest, grazed on the grass and found it delicious. From time to time, with a shake of his head or tail, he chased the flies that were bothering him.

The tiger came up close to him. He observed the monster, who did not see him and went right on grazing.

"I really would like to know what else he can do," the tiger said to himself. "This animal doesn't seem so terrible to me!"

At that moment, as if to show what he could do, the monster abruptly raised his head and began to bray. He brayed three times very, very loudly! The tiger, who had never before heard such a noise, thought it was a signal that the monster was going to devour him. He was so afraid that he fled immediately.

But as he did not know to whom he could tell what he had seen and heard, and since he really wanted to know what this monster was capable of, the tiger did not go far. He remained hidden in the forest and waited.

Soon he heard the animal bray again. He heard it several times, and after a while he became used to the noise. When he was no longer afraid of it at all, he moved closer to the strange animal. Soon the tiger was walking right up to the monster.

The monster saw him coming, but since he had never met a tiger, he was not afraid either, and he didn't think of running away.

The tiger just touched the monster's leg to see what he could do. The monster, startled and a little annoyed, answered with a kick of his foot.

The tiger received the blow. He found that it didn't hurt him very much at all! He waited a little, then he struck the stranger with a swish of his tail to see what he would do.

The monster wanted to be left alone, and he gave the tiger a swift kick. The tiger again felt that he was not hurt too badly. He approached the monster once again and this time gave him a good blow with his paw. The monster, who was now very angry, began again to kick and strike the tiger with his hooves.

"Then that is all he knows how to do," concluded the tiger. "He only knows how to eat grass, bray, and kick. It really isn't worthwhile eating him!"

And letting out a terrible roar to show the monster that he, the tiger, was truly the strongest animal in the forest of Tian, he went to tell the monkey and the fox that this monster was only a donkey after all!

The House Of Blue Porcelain

There was in the village of Lang Wou a strange house of blue porcelain in which nobody lived. No one knew to whom it belonged, and for a long time no one dared enter it, because the people of the village thought that a family of genies had taken over the house.

The young lord Wang Li was both curious and brave; he had proved this on more than one occasion. His friends, who were very intrigued by this mysterious house, agreed among themselves to talk to him about it and make him curious enough to go there.

"Strange things seem to take place in the house of blue porcelain," they kept telling him. "It seems that sometimes music and echoes of voices are heard around it and perfumes seem to come from it."

"I don't believe a thing!" always responded Lord Wang Li, laughing. "I only believe what I see!"

"You are wrong," his friends answered him. "The genies, who are invisible beings, can work wonders."

"You will not convince me. Genies do not exist!" the young lord repeated stubbornly. "And I bet you there is no one in that empty house!"

"Well then, go there to be sure, and then we will believe you!" retorted the friends of Wang Li, whose curiosity was now awakened.

"All right!" he finally said. "Since you insist, I am going to visit your genies!"

Followed by his servants and his companions, the young lord started out for the house of blue porcelain. He went up to the door with them and knocked. As the peephole in the door was half opened, Wang Li passed his visiting card through it and waited. Soon the door opened wide for him, although he could not see anyone. He turned around and realized that his servants and friends had fled in fright.

But, not the least bit afraid, Wang Li entered. He went down the length of a hall that led to a vast reception room, the door of which opened all by itself in front of him. There still was no one near him, but he noticed that the room was richly furnished and decorated. He walked towards a sofa covered with silk, and said in a loud voice as he bowed, "Whoever you are, sir or madam, I greet you and thank you for your hospitality. Now would you please be so kind as to let me see your face and speak to me!"

"I cannot show myself to you," answered the voice of a young man very close to him. "But sit down beside me, for we are going to have some tea and talk together. I am very happy that you have come to visit me!"

With that, two cushions came over to the low table, and a red lacquer tray on which were fine porcelain cups came and placed itself on the table.

Wang Li, astonished, realized that an invisible hand was raising the teapot. He bent toward his cup, which became filled with a deliciously perfumed tea, while the plates became covered with honey cakes and sweetmeats.

The tea was exquisite, and the cakes delicious. An agreeable conversation began between young Lord Wang Li and his invisible host, who seemed extremely pleasant.

While chatting thus, Wang Li said to himself, "I will tell my friends about this amazing visit and this elegant tea party! They will willingly believe my strange adventure, since they are convinced that genies exist and that they live in this house of blue porcelain."

However when Lord Wang Li, after having politely taken leave of his host, found his friends and told them about his afternoon, they took him for a young man with a vivid imagination and a gift for comedy. They would not believe a word he said. At last Wang Li began asking himself if he had not been dreaming.

But the following day held new surprises for him. Lord Wang Li had not told his friends that the mysterious inhabitant of the house of blue porcelain had invited him for lunch for the next day. He arrived at the agreed upon hour, and this time he felt he was really expected. Many invisible servants busied themselves around him, and he was soon seated in front of the low table. He hardly had time to think, "I would really like to eat some turtle meat with seven sauces," when the desired dish appeared before him. And thus, all during the meal, invisible servants brought him wines, fruits, and all the foods that he wished for!

All the time he was eating, Wang Li carried on a pleasant conversation with his new friend, whose presence he felt alongside him. But the young man wanted to know more about his host so that he might be able to convince his friends.

Finally he said to him, "Even though I am not permitted to see you, might I at least know your name, generous host?"

"My servants call me Lord Precious Jade, although that is not my name. I cannot reveal to you my family name because, as you must realize, I am a genie!"

When Wang Li reported this conversation to his friends, they did not know whether to believe him or not. However, they did not dare make fun of him and, curiously, not one of them wanted to accompany him on these mysterious meetings.

Wang Li did not care, and he made it a habit to go to the house of blue porcelain and visit his invisible friend several times a week. Together they recited poems, spoke of thousands of things, and discussed literature, science, and art. It seemed to Lord Wang Li that his mysterious friend had a great deal of knowledge on all subjects.

43245

One day he said to him, "Dear Precious Jade, you have the voice of a young man, and you could be my age, but your knowledge far surpasses mine and that of my constant companions, who are really very well educated. Would it be possible for you to tell me your age?"

"That is, unfortunately, a question which I cannot answer for you, dear Lord Wang Li, and besides I stopped counting my years a long time ago," answered the learned genie. "Do not be shocked if I tell you that I am more than a thousand years old! That should explain to you how I know so many things."

Young Wang Li was speechless with surprise! When he left the house of blue porcelain, he went straight to his friends and told them what had happened. But his friends refused to believe him.

"How can we believe in doors that open mysteriously before you, cushions that move by themselves, and tables that produce delicious food at your wish? You must prove to us the existence of this learned genie who says he is more than a thousand years old!"

That evening, as soon as Wang Li greeted his invisible friend, Precious Jade, who seemed to be able to read the thoughts of the young man, said to him, "Lord Wang Li, may I know the worries that seem to be bothering you? If you have not been able to leave them at the door of my house of porcelain, is it perhaps because they concern me? I would like to please you because I am very grateful for your faithful friendship. If I can do anything at all to help you, I wish you would tell me."

"My dear Precious Jade," admitted Wang Li, "I have often spoken of you to my friends. As a matter of fact, it was they who sent me here, because they wanted to know if your house was really inhabited by genies. But now that we meet so often and have become friends, I cannot convince them of your existence!"

There was a long silence. Young Wang Li feared that he had made his friend Precious Jade angry, and since he could not see his face, it was not easy to know what he was thinking.

"Let us see," Precious Jade finally said in his usual tone, "what can we do?"

"May I propose an idea to you?" inquired Wang Li, who was still worried.

"I have told you, I have only one purpose — to please you in order to prove my gratitude to you. If I am able to convince your friends, it will be a satisfaction for me also," declared the genie.

"At the edge of the village," began Wang Li, "there is a terrible old woman whom some people call Servant of the Devil. This sorceress goes from one sick person to another, asking for money, precious objects, or jewels, in exchange for supposedly magic remedies. When she can no longer get anything from the sick person, she abandons him to his sad lot."

"I know this woman. She is evil in person!" cried Precious Jade. "The people cannot defend themselves against her because the greatest misfortunes befall those who resist her. But it is in my power to combat her evil spells."

"Then help me to conquer her!" exclaimed Wang Li. "The whole village will be grateful to you, and my companions will finally believe in your existence."

Precious Jade clapped his hands, and a saddled horse was immediately brought to the front door. The door opened for Wang Li, who wondered what he should do.

Precious Jade anticipated his question and said to him, "Mount this horse and go to the old woman. My power accompanies you and my servants are at your command!"

After thanking him, Wang Li went away on horseback to the other end of the village where the horrible Servant of the Devil lived. As he galloped along, Wang Li noticed several specks of dust on his sleeve, and as he went to brush them off with the back of his hand, he heard a voice murmur in his ear, "No, do not do that. We are servants of Lord Precious Jade. We have orders to accompany you and to help you."

Wang Li soon arrived at the old woman's house. He dismounted and entered. The wicked sorceress received him with a smile, happy to see a rich man come into her house.

"How does it happen," she asked, "that a noble lord comes to see a woman as poor as I am? Of what ills might I have the pleasure of curing you, sir?"

But her face changed when Wang Li spoke severely to her, looking her straight in the eyes.

"I have heard that you intend to return all the money that you have taken from the poor people of the village. I have come to help you with this task."

"That is out of the question!" screamed the sorceress. "You do not know my power, young man, or you wouldn't dare speak to me like that." And the Servant of the Devil started to mutter strange words.

Then Wang Li remembered the specks of dust that remained on his sleeve. He shook his arms saying, "Servants of Lord Precious Jade, can you help me?"

Immediately, a cloud of dust enveloped the woman, who began to choke.

"Help! Stop suffocating me!" The Servant of the Devil could hardly make herself heard.

"Now do you understand a little better what I mean?" Wang Li asked dryly.

"Yes I understand!" said the woman, catching her breath, while the specks of dust came back and placed themselves on the sleeve of Wang Li's tunic. "But these riches have been given to me willingly in exchange for my magic remedies."

"You are lying!" answered Wang Li, again shaking his sleeve.

A cloud of dust, thicker and blacker, enveloped the woman's head and she thought she was dying. She was barely able to whisper, "Take back everything! But just let me breathe!"

The cloud, becoming white dust once more, again placed itself on the tunic of Wang Li, who cried out to the sorceress, "Where is the money?"

"In that chest," answered the old woman, pointing to it.

Wang Li raised the cover of a large rustic wooden chest. It was completely filled with gold and silver, lengths of silk, objects of wood, carved ivory, and precious stones. He unrolled a long piece of paper on which were noted in the handwriting of the sorceress the names of all the people of the village whose goods she had taken.

When Wang Li finished reading the long list, a terrible clap of thunder surprised him! He found himself alone in the road with the treasure chest before him. The sorceress and her house had disappeared!

The joy of the inhabitants of the village was indescribable! Each one came to take back his possessions and express his gratitude to Lord Wang Li. But Wang Li proclaimed that he had only been the instrument of the genie known as Lord Precious Jade, who lived in the house of blue porcelain.

Forthwith, the villagers went to place offerings of gratitude at the door of the house of blue porcelain, but no one wanted to enter into it. Young Lord Wang Li alone had the privilege of passing more and more frequent and happy moments there, while his bonds of friendship with Precious Jade became stronger every day.

Of course Wang Li's companions were now convinced of the existence of the mysterious and kind genie.

It would soon be a year since Wang Li began going regularly to the house of blue porcelain. One evening the dinner with his invisible friend went on longer and later than usual. His mysterious host started to speak in a sad voice that Wang Li had never heard him use before.

"Dear friend, we must separate from each other now, for I can no longer stay in this place."

Wang Li was grieved to learn that he would have to give up the pleasure of listening to this invisible companion with

whom he had shared so many joys for almost a year. He remained silent, not knowing how to express his grief.

Precious Jade added, "You have been a true friend, one such as genies never meet. You have kept me company without ever complaining about not seeing me, and without asking anything for yourself. This evening I am going to show you my face so that you can recognize me if destiny permits our paths to cross again!"

With this, there appeared in front of Wang Li a young man of perfect beauty, who looked at him smiling. He was dressed in a tunic of purple silk embroidered all over with gold and precious stones. The vision lasted for only a single instant, but Wang Li knew he would never forget the face of his friend.

Then he found himself alone, seated on the ground in a house entirely empty, abandoned, in which not even a spirit lived.

Years passed and Wang Li's life became more difficult. He was no longer very young nor as rich as he had been. The memory of his strange friendship with a being whom he had only been able to see for an instant became an almost forgotten dream.

Actually, Wang Li was no longer rich at all, for from year to year his wealth had diminished. However, he continued to share what he had with a younger brother who without his help, would not have even the necessities of life.

One evening, coming back from the Capital where he had just met his brother, Lord Wang Li's heart was heavy and he felt deeply discouraged. A nimble horseman passed him on the road, then turned around and greeted him courteously. They rode along together for a while, speaking of one thing or another. Wang Li did not, of course, unburden his troubles to the horseman. However, he felt himself strangely moved by this man who made him relive in his mind the almost forgotten memories of his happy youth.

The face of the young man reminded him of someone he might have met before. This face expressed more than sympathy, and Wang Li had the fleeting impression that he was speaking to someone he knew—to a friend, perhaps?

"You seem preoccupied, sir," his traveling companion said to him kindly. "May I know why?"

"Young lord," answered Wang Li, "I can tell you my troubles if you wish me to, but I do not think that they could possibly be of interest to you. I once was a young man, rich and happy, spoiled by the good life, and now I am older and quite poor. My brother and I share what I have left, and soon that will not be enough to live on."

Contrary to what Wang Li expected, the young man appeared to be interested in his troubles. When they had to sepa-

rate at a crossroad, Wang Li already felt much better—in fact he felt almost happy.

"Sir Wang Li," the horseman said to him before turning away, "you will soon meet an old man who will give you a gift. I pray you to accept it willingly."

Wang Li, very surprised, wanted to ask for some explanation, but the horseman had already ridden away at a great gallop before Wang Li had even thought to ask him his name.

A few minutes later, Wang Li noticed an old man walking down the other side of the road carrying a little casket. The old man crossed the road, and bowed in front of Wang Li. Putting the little casket in Wang Li's hands, he said, "From Lord Precious Jade to his friend Lord Wang Li."

Wang Li immediately got off his horse and wished to thank the old man, but he had already disappeared. When Wang Li opened the casket, he was astonished to find that it was filled with pieces of gold and silver!

Hoping that his faithful friend, who had become invisible again, would be able to hear him, Wang Li cried out with tears in his eyes. Then he shook the three specks of dust that had just appeared on his sleeve and said, "Go and thank my friend Precious Jade on my behalf. I did not recognize him, but I have not forgotten him and I never will forget him!"

The Revenge of the Little Rabbit

Hou Ping Pang was a little white rabbit who lived next to a big, powerful, and ferocious lion. What a haughty and vain neighbor was this lion, Chong Chang! Everyone on the mountain knew how unpleasant he was.

He always bragged about his strength in front of the little rabbit, made fun of him on every occasion, and always looked down at him scornfully.

One day, the lion went so far as to insult Hou Ping Pang. He even threatened him because the little rabbit, forgetting all the usual bowing and scraping, had dared to take three leaps in front of the lion's house.

This time Hou Ping Pang, truly angry, decided that he would get even with his arrogant neighbor. The next time the little rabbit met the lion, he gave him a strange piece of news, which immediately made the lion very angry.

"Oh great lion, Chong Chang," the rabbit said to him, "do you know whom I met on the other side of the mountain?"

"No," answered the great lion, who lent an inattentive ear to what little Hou Ping Pang had to say.

"I have discovered an extraordinary person who is exactly like you!" exclaimed the little rabbit.

"Ah? And what did he say?" asked the lion, gruffly.

"He said to me, 'It is I who am the strongest! I am the biggest and most powerful! If anyone believes he is stronger than I, let him come and compare himself to me. If not, he will have to obey me and serve me!'" reported the rabbit.

"And you did not even tell him about me, stupid rabbit?" roared Chong Chang, who was already fuming with rage.

"Oh but I did, and as a matter of fact, it would have been better if I had kept quiet. When I talked to him about your strength and your power, he started to laugh. He dared to make fun of you! He contended that you were surely not even worthy to be his servant!" said the rabbit.

Then the great lion, Chong Chang, roared with anger, "What! Where is this animal? Where is he who says he is stronger than I, and whom I can kill with one blow of my paw?"

"On the other side of the mountain, Sir Lion!" said the rabbit, Hou Ping Pang, jumping around in front of the lion. "I can even take you there if you do not believe me. Besides, he's waiting for you to show you . . ."

"Let's go there at once!" roared the lion, interrupting Hou Ping Pang, and he dashed after the little rabbit. "He will learn who is the King of the Animals, who is the greatest, the strongest, the most . . ."

In his anger the arrogant Chong Chang could not find any more words important enough to describe himself. He also began to get out of breath running behind Hou Ping Pang, who ran on ahead of him and of whom he was constantly losing sight.

The clever little rabbit deliberately made lots of turns and detours to tire the lion, always managing to keep a good distance from the furious animal.

Finally, toward evening, Hou Ping Pang showed the lion a well in the distance and said to him, "Oh, Sir Lion, the one who dares to say he is more powerful than you lives there, at the bottom of that well. He is waiting for you! Will you dare confront him?"

At these words, the furious lion ran up to the well, while Hou Ping Pang remained crouching in the bushes. The lion, Chong Chang, leaned his two front legs on the edge of the well and threw a fierce look inside. The same fierce look was staring up at him from the bottom of the well!

Then the lion, Chong Chang, let out a ferocious roar to intimidate his adversary, "ARRRROUUUUGH!"

"ARRRROUUUUGH!" answered the animal from the bottom of the well with just as much strength and fury.

The lion grimaced in rage, and his adversary grimaced in the same way. The lion showed his terrible teeth and his opponent showed his, which were just exactly as terrible.

Then the lion, Chong Chang, his mane bristling with rage, flung out his front legs to show that he wanted to fight, and he roared even louder, "ARRRROUUUUUUGH! ARRRROUUUUUUGH!" His frightful roar echoed in the well.

But immediately afterward, a clear and joyous laugh answered him from behind the bushes, and Hou Ping Pang, the little rabbit, took off at top speed.

Only then did the arrogant, the powerful, the great lion, Chong Chang, realize that little Hou Ping Pang had tricked him by bringing him so far simply to show him his image in the bottom of a well where there was nothing but water!

The lion was so embarrassed at having allowed himself to be tricked by a rabbit that he remained on the other side of the mountain, leaving little Hou Ping Pang to live in peace.

The One Hundred Thousand Arrows of K'ong Ming

In the time of the Three Kingdoms, two generals regularly confronted each other from opposite banks of the Long River. Their names were General Ts'ao Ts'ao and General Tcheou Yu. It was almost always Tcheou Yu who won the battles because he was especially sly, and he knew how to use the most skillful stratagems against the tactics of his adversary.

However, after each one of his victories, General Tcheou Yu was a little suspicious of his counselor, K'ong Ming. Because of his intelligence, K'ong Ming was becoming very troublesome! He succeeded in learning the most secret plans devised by his general well before these plans were revealed. He seemed to guess, as if by magic, the most daring moves planned by his superior. No one knew how he was able to discover all these things.

One day, an officer of General Tcheou Yu came to report to him that his counselor already knew his next plan. K'ong Ming had even gone so far as to discuss the plan publicly and make fun of it.

This time General Tcheou Yu's fury knew no bounds. He shouted angrily, "That is enough! It is time I got rid of this counselor!"

His officers warned him that K'ong Ming would probably go immediately to serve as counselor to the enemy, General Ts'ao Ts'ao, on the other side of the Long River. But General Tcheou Yu had an idea, which he had no intention of revealing. He whispered into his beard, "I will find a good reason to have him put to death!"

The general had already thought of a way to go about it; but all he said to his officers was, "Do not ask me anything now. You will soon see!"

The next day General Tcheou Yu called together his staff to announce to them that he intended to attack his enemy, General Ts'ao Ts'ao, on the river. Then, turning politely towards his counselor, K'ong Ming, he addressed himself to him.

"In your opinion," he asked him, "what weapons should we use for this naval combat?"

"Arrows, my general, without a doubt!" answered K'ong Ming, who knew, however, that the army of Tcheou Yu did not have any arrows left after its last battle.

"That is my opinion also," said the general with a satisfied air. "But at this moment we do not possess a sufficient quantity. I am asking you to procure for me one hundred thousand arrows very quickly, because this naval combat must take place with as short a delay as possible."

"When do you need these arrows, my general?" inquired K'ong Ming, without appearing to be the least upset.

"Within ten days at the latest!" the general answered curtly, knowing full well that he thus demanded of his coun-

selor an impossible task that would cost K'ong Ming his life, because death was the punishment for not obeying an order.

"Ten days will be too late!" answered K'ong Ming. "The army of General Ts'ao Ts'ao will have already attacked us!"

Tcheou Yu wondered how his counselor could know so well the intentions of the enemy, but he said nothing about it to K'ong Ming.

"Very well," he replied, without showing any emotion. "When can you deliver the arrows to me?"

"In three days, my general!" declared K'ong Ming.

That seemed like a joke. All the officers, thunderstruck on hearing this response, jumped up and waited in silence to hear what the general, who could hardly conceal his astonishment, was going to say.

"I am giving you the official order!" he finally exclaimed. "In three days you will deliver to me the one hundred thousand arrows!"

Actually, General Tcheou Yu was not unhappy. His plan was unfolding even better than he had hoped. For a moment he had thought it was insolence or a trick on the part of his counselor, but it was clear now that K'ong Ming had taken a wrong step. He would not come out of this alive!

"Three days from tomorrow morning, you will receive the one hundred thousand arrows!" promised K'ong Ming.

General Tcheou Yu was jubilant. He was convinced that his counselor had just signed his own death warrant. He would never be able to obtain the arrows in such a short time. But this attitude did not prevent the general from going to see the people who were usually responsible for cutting and shaping the stalks of bamboo from which they made arrows.

"Above all," he said to them, "do not obey my counselor when he comes with an urgent order for an improbable quantity of arrows! He is much too zealous! As a matter of fact, take all the time necessary to prepare and deliver them. There is no rush."

At the same time, K'ong Ming asked his friend, Colonel Lou Sou, to come to see him with his officers.

"General Tcheou Yu wants to kill me," he said to them. "But if you secretly do exactly what I'm going to tell you, within three days we will deliver to him the one hundred thousand arrows."

"And how will we do that?" inquired Colonel Lou Sou, very much intrigued.

"Prepare twenty large barges with flat bottoms. Each one will have to carry a crew of thirty men who must be kept ready to embark. They must take on board with them everything that can make noise or music. On the bulwarks of these boats, have them pile up bales of straw to a height of more than two meters. Cover the straw with a cloth of midnight blue and await my further orders."

Colonel Lou Sou did not dare to ask for explanations in spite of his curiosity. He had confidence in K'ong Ming, whose intelligence and skill he had known for a long time.

So in the greatest secrecy the colonel had twenty large barges prepared and loaded with straw, just as K'ong Ming had ordered. During this time the six hundred men were preparing to embark.

But what was K'ong Ming, whose life was now in danger, doing? The general staff of General Tcheou Yu observed him with astonishment. The first day the counselor stayed at home, calmly playing checkers with his friends and listening to music.

And the second day when everyone, friend or adversary, waited to see him go out and act at last, he busied himself drinking wine and having a good time.

When General Tcheou Yu learned of this, he started to laugh and declared to his supporters, "He is right to take his time! Let him take advantage of it, for in a few days he will be condemned to death!"

However, the following night well before sunrise, K'ong Ming arose and sent for Colonel Lou Sou, who came to him immediately.

"The hour has come to go look for our arrows!" K'ong Ming said to him after the customary greetings.

"And where do you expect to obtain them?" asked Lou Sou.

"You will soon understand," K'ong Ming assured him calmly, taking care not to say anything more just yet.

One hour later twenty long barges tied together crossed the Long River in silence, heading towards the opposite bank, up to the camp of the enemy, General Ts'ao Ts'ao. The night was dark and the fog dense. The fleet progressed, but remained invisible.

As soon as he saw the lights of the enemy's campfires, K'ong Ming gave the order to all the men to make a frightful noise.

"And now," he cried to them, "beat your war drums! Clap your cymbals! Bang your pots and iron bars and scream as hard as you can to surprise the enemy!"

"But what if they attack us?" gasped Colonel Lou Sou, who had not yet caught on to the trick. "We haven't an arrow with which to defend ourselves!"

"In this fog, they will not dare take to their ships. Come on, keep up the racket!" K'ong Ming cried out to the men.

General Ts'ao Ts'ao did indeed give the order to his soldiers to rush to the bank of the river and shoot their arrows at the assailants. But his soldiers could only distinguish vague forms moving slowly back and forth on the barges under the inexhaustible rain of arrows.

When the sun finally dissipated the fog, the boats, bristling with all of General Ts'ao Ts'ao's arrows, went right up alongside General Ts'ao Ts'ao's camp, K'ong Ming's men saluting as they thanked the enemy for the arrows! Safe behind their arrow-pierced bales of straw, the men began again to beat their drums and clap their cymbals.

Now all they had to do was to count the arrows they had received. There were more than one hundred thousand of them! General Tcheou Yu learned when he awoke that he had lost the contest of wits with his wise counselor, K'ong Ming.

Colonel Lou Sou had one more question to ask of K'ong Ming, in whom he was proud to have had confidence.

"May I know," he said to him, "how you were able to foresee that there would be so much fog until sunrise?"

"Because I am a great strategist," K'ong Ming answered him. "General Tcheou Yu wanted to get rid of me, but a great strategist knows all the secrets of the sky and the earth! If I asked for three days delay, it was just because I knew there would be fog this morning!"

The Three Treasures of Tchou-ti

Poor Tchou-ti was a simple and loyal boy, but he had an empty mind, empty as a rice field after the harvest. Everyone thought he was a fool. His courage was hardly anything to brag about, but his foolishness was famous!

"I'm afraid that this boy will never be capable of bringing the tiniest amount of money into the house," lamented his mother. "He knows how to do absolutely nothing!"

One day, exasperated by her do-nothing son, his mother gave him a box of biscuits and a bag filled with food and sent him out.

"Look, Tchou-ti," she said to him, "here is enough food to feed you for several days. And now, you're on your own. Do not come back to the house until you have earned some money."

Tchou-ti went away walking straight ahead, grieved at
having to leave his home. And how can one earn money when
one does not know how to do anything? Sick at heart, the boy
walked aimlessly and by chance arrived at the edge of a
stream where he sat down to rest and nibble on biscuits.

As he was idly daydreaming while looking at the bank of
the stream, he noticed a small bluish-green snake no longer
than a chopstick. It seemed to be staring at Tchou-ti, and it
remained there without moving, as if it were sick or starved.

Tchou-ti took pity on the snake. He got up, took it carefully
in his hands, and laid it on the grass alongside him. He gave it
a biscuit, then two, then three.

The little bluish-green serpent visibly gained strength.
When there was only a single biscuit left, Tchou-ti put the ser-

pent on a bed of bamboo leaves in a little box and decided that it would be his companion. He would take it along with him on his mission to earn money and make his mother happy.

But very quickly Tchou-ti's box became too small for the serpent, which had grown quite long. The boy had to bring it back to the edge of the stream where he had found it, and the serpent allowed him to do so. But day after day, Tchou-ti continued to feed the snake, bringing it melon seeds, hearts of bamboo, and the last bits of food that were left in his bag.

Time passed, and the boy still had not found a way to bring money into the house. He wondered if he should try to sell his snake in the market, although he had grown very fond of it and had no desire to lose it.

One day, seeing Tchou-ti come toward him, the serpent, who had become really enormous, said to him, "Tchou-ti, take me now to the edge of the Long River. I am dying of boredom here."

"Well," confessed Tchou-ti, who did not know how to hide his thoughts, "I really wanted to sell you at the market. Since I have not earned any money, my mother will not want me back at the house, and I would so much like to go back home."

The snake looked at him a moment and said, "Do not worry any longer, Tchou-ti, earning money is easy! I promise to make you rich. But first take me to the Long River."

Then Tchou-ti, who was usually so lazy, quickly wove a large basket out of cane. He put the snake in the basket, put the basket on his back, and hurried to the river. They had barely arrived when the snake plunged into the water. Tchou-ti watched it disappear, thoughtfully wondering if it would keep its promise.

Suddenly the serpent rose to the top of the water and, in front of the astonished boy, was transformed into a magnificent blue dragon with golden scales and powerful claws. For a moment the dragon swayed in the waves under the eyes of the amazed Tchou-ti, then he stood up out of the water and exclaimed, "Tchou-ti, you saved my life! You have fed me; you have carried me in your hands, then in your arms, and finally on your back. I promised you that I would make you rich. Well then, take the little donkey that is waiting for you on the river bank. I give it to you as a treasure. If you wish some gold, simply say to it, 'Little Burro, if you please, make me some gold,' and he will make as much as you wish! If you want money for your mother, say to him, 'Little Burro, if you please, make me some money,' and he will immediately make as much of it as you ask him for. But be careful, Tchou-ti, do not tell a single soul about this!"

And even before the dumbfounded boy had time to thank him, the dragon disappeared in a great undertow, and there was a little donkey waiting for its master on the bank of the river. Tchou-ti caught it by its halter. He wanted to start home at once, for he could hardly wait to show his mother what the little donkey could do. But night was already falling, and the house of Tchou-ti was still half a day's journey away.

Fortunately the boy came upon an inn by the side of the road, and he knocked on the door. The innkeeper hurried to welcome Tchou-ti and wished to take his little donkey to the stable.

"Take good care of him!" foolish Tchou-ti cried out, incapable of keeping a secret, "because he is not at all an ordinary donkey! Give him some fresh straw and feed him well. But especially — especially — do not say to him, 'Little Burro, if you please, make me some gold;' or, 'Little Burro, if you please, make me some money.' "

Naturally the innkeeper promised that he would ask nothing of the little donkey, but would give him the best of care. He put the donkey into the stable and gave him some fresh straw. Then he showed Tchou-ti to his room and, with much bowing and scraping, bade him goodnight.

But the man had heard Tchou-ti's foolish words very clearly and he remembered them well. For half the night they went round and round in his head, and at the hour of the rat, which

begins before midnight, he could stand it no longer. The good man got up, took a lamp, lit it, and headed straight for the stable. He opened its door without a sound.

"Ha'ya!" he said amicably to the little donkey, patting its back to wake it up. "Little Burro, if you please, make me some gold!"

He had scarcely finished saying these words when he saw tumbling down before the donkey, a whole pile of gold pieces glittering in the light of the lamp!

"By Buddha!" he said to himself, "under my own roof I have a donkey that makes gold. I'm not going to let it go just like that! I am going to get my own little donkey and put it in the place of this animal. And then I will hide the little burro who makes gold. Tchou-ti will never know the difference!"

And well before daybreak, the innkeeper went joyously back to bed, having exchanged the two animals without being noticed. He had carefully hidden the gold in his rice jar and the magic donkey in a little hut behind his house.

At the hour of the rabbit—between 5 and 6 o'clock in the morning—Tchou-ti was up and ready to leave. The innkeeper lavished much attention on him, brought him the little donkey, and wished him a good journey, with more bowing and scraping.

When his mother saw her son arrive with a little donkey, she exclaimed, "I am happy to see you, Tchou-ti. But why do you bring me a donkey? Did I not ask you to bring us back some money?"

"Mother," cried the boy, "do not complain. I bring you a treasure! Just give me a brand new mat, and my little donkey will make some gold for you."

The mother, astonished, hurried to stretch out a nice mat on the ground. Tchou-ti led the donkey to it and while patting its back he kept repeating, "Little Burro, if you please, make me some gold!" The little burro had his four feet well on the mat, but he did nothing, absolutely nothing! He did not seem to understand what was being said to him.

"Little Burro, if you please, make me some money— please!" Tchou-ti asked of him, now very worried. But the donkey shook its ears impatiently and did nothing.

"You see! You see! He will do nothing!" lamented his mother.

"You must wait yet, mother. I tell you that he is going to make us some gold."

"You naughty child, unworthy son!" cried his mother, furious. "How dare you play such a trick on your poor mother! Get out of here with your donkey and may I never see you again!"

So Tchou-ti started out again, dragging the little donkey behind him. The poor boy felt terribly sad and full of bitterness toward the dragon who had made him false promises. He headed straight for the Long River to accuse the dragon of telling him a lie.

Tchou-ti arrived at the edge of the river just before sunset. Immediately an enormous wave formed and the magnificent dragon emerged from the billows. Again, in spite of his anger, the boy was dazzled by the beauty of the blue dragon with the golden scales.

"Why did you come to see me, Tchou-ti?" asked the dragon.

"Take back your donkey, which makes neither gold nor money!" cried Tchou-ti, resentfully. "Because of it I have once again been chased out of my house."

"If you do not want a little donkey, that is all right. I will give you something else," the dragon answered patiently, without trying to justify himself. "Do you want the tablecloth that is waiting for you at the edge of the river?"

"What shall I do with a tablecloth, dragon? I have neither house, nor table, nor anything to eat!" cried Tchou-ti, still very angry.

"Listen to me, Tchou-ti!" said the dragon, "when you are hungry, spread out this tablecloth wherever you wish and three times in a loud voice ask for all the food you want. It will serve you the food immediately. Go bring this tablecloth to your mother, but do not speak to anyone about it—no one!"

The boy thanked the dragon, took the tablecloth nicely folded on his arm, and once again started out towards his home. But as it was completely dark by now, he had to knock once again at the door of the inn.

When the innkeeper saw him arrive, he rolled his eyes in fright. Was this the boy whose magic donkey he had stolen standing before him? He must have come back to punish him! It certainly was he, but the boy did not ask anything of him except a bed and a corner in which to sleep until the next morning.

"And above all," he told the innkeeper, "above all, do not take advantage of my sleep to order from this magic table-cloth all the food that you would like!"

The innkeeper, always smiling, backed out of the room where Tchou-ti was to sleep. He wished him goodnight as he bowed to the ground, assuring him that for all the gold in the world, he would not touch his tablecloth!

But now the man knew that the tablecloth was magic, and at once he made a plan.

As soon as the boy was asleep, he came to steal the tablecloth, which he replaced with one that he took out of his own cupboard and which was exactly like the magic cloth. Then the innkeeper went back to his own room, and commanded, "Tablecloth, magic tablecloth, bring me a soup of bamboo shoots, some lamb with seven sauces, a bowl of rice, a slice of watermelon, and an almond cake!"

Immediately the tablecloth in front of the amazed innkeeper was covered with everything he had ordered. When he had eaten it all, the man fell into such a deep sleep that he did not even hear Tchou-ti get up and leave at the crow of the cock, the ordinary tablecloth nicely folded under his arm.

And when Tchou-ti's mother saw him arrive carrying the tablecloth, she exclaimed, "My son, why do you bring this tablecloth to the house? We have absolutely nothing to put on it."

"Mother," said the boy, "this is not an ordinary tablecloth. I am going to spread it out and ask for all the food you desire, and it will serve it to you!"

And addressing the tablecloth, Tchou-ti commanded, "Tablecloth, magic tablecloth, bring us some rice!"

But in vain he insisted, repeated, ordered again and again, and even became angry; not a grain of rice appeared on the tablecloth.

His mother, beside herself, grabbed her son, gave him a scolding, and not wishing to hear any of his explanations, chased him once again out of the house.

So Tchou-ti found himself on the road once more. He could not understand why the dragon had made him so many false promises. He felt terribly unhappy and full of bitterness towards the dragon, who had lied to him again.

He arrived at the edge of the Long River just before nightfall. Immediately a large wave formed and the dragon

emerged from the billows, more beautiful than ever in the light of the setting sun.

"Why are you returning again to see me? And what can I do for you, Tchou-ti?"

"Dragon, once again you have tricked me. The tablecloth that you gave me did not make the tiniest grain of rice appear for my mother and me. Why do you take pleasure in making fun of me?"

"Bad luck to that innkeeper!" said the dragon. "Since it's like that, I am going to give you something else."

And he put into Tchou-ti's hand a thick, solid club, saying, "Tonight you must warn the innkeeper that he absolutely must not say to the club, 'Club, club, hit me very hard!' Whatever happens, do not forget to say this to the innkeeper."

With the club on his shoulder, Tchou-ti returned to the inn for the third time. On seeing him come with his club, the innkeeper rolled his eyes, even more frightened than the last evening. Had he not hidden the little donkey that made gold and money and put away in his chest the magic tablecloth that brought him all the food he desired?

But the boy, tired as usual, asked him only for a mat and a corner in which to sleep until dawn. Before lying down, he did not forget to say to the man, "And above all, above all — do not come in while I am sleeping and say to this magic club beside me, 'Club, club, hit me very hard!' "

"Why of course not," promised the innkeeper, always all smiles and bows. "I wouldn't do anything like that."

But at the hour of the rat, when everyone else was asleep, the innkeeper got up once again, and without even lighting his lamp, went to look for the club alongside of the sleeping Tchou-ti.

Without thinking, as soon as he arrived in the room, the man repeated the magic phrase that the boy had given him, "Club, club, hit me very hard!"

Hardly had these words escaped his lips, when the club bounded out of his hands and — BANG — gave him a terrible blow on his skull. BANG and BAM — the club hit the innkeeper all over his body. It beat him unmercifully, following him as he ran through the house and finally back to the room where Tchou-ti was still sleeping. And while the blows fell heavily on his back, the innkeeper started to beg Tchou-ti, "Help! Quick! Have mercy! Take back your club! Take it back or I will die! I will give you back your little donkey that makes gold and your magic tablecloth, for it is I who stole them from you."

Immediately, the club stopped beating him. Completely flabbergasted, Tchou-ti once again headed home, but this time with three real treasures — a little donkey that really made gold and a tablecloth that really served the best of foods. As for the club, he never again had any need for it.

Tchou-ti returned sometimes to the Long River to see the dragon at sunset because he loved him, but he never again had to ask him for anything.

The Little Yellow Dragon against the Big Black Dragon

On the shore of Lake Eul, not far from the city of Tali in Yun Nan Province, there lived a mother and her son. The little boy was called Dragon of Yun Nan, and only his mother knew the secret of his extraordinary birth. This child without a father was born from a dragon pearl. Before the child's birth, a phoenix, the exotic bird that always prophesies a unique destiny, came and rested on the roof of the cottage. And the instant the baby was born, this fabulous bird spread its multicolored wings, which were as beautiful as a painted screen.

However, up until he was ten years old nothing distinguished the boy from the other children, and his mother waited.

Then one year misfortune came to Lake Eul and its banks, for the big Black Dragon who lived in the lake suddenly noticed that he was missing one of his precious robes—the most beautiful one of all!

He began to toss about, stirring up the waters of the lake and growling loudly, "Where is my robe—my robe of water lily petals?"

"How should I know?" his wife answered him, disappearing into the deep water.

Then the dragon really became furious. He started to leap high out of the water, causing such turbulence that the boats of several fishermen sank to the bottom of the lake.

Actually, the wife of the Black Dragon was lying. It was she who had helped the White Dragon, whom she secretly loved, to hide the precious robe.

The big Black Dragon, angrier and angrier, growled like thunder for several weeks. And since he still could not find his robe, he blocked the two canals through which the waters of the lake flowed, so that he could search the lake from top to bottom. The level of the water immediately started to rise dangerously. It rose more each day, and flood threatened the banks of the lake.

However, the big Black Dragon kept hunting for his robe throughout the lake, making enormous waves that submerged the rice fields and threatened to drown the inhabitants. The water had risen so high that the bridge, called Bridge of the Dragon, became impassable and the people on the opposite bank were cut off from everything.

One day, coming back from the fields, young Dragon of Yun Nan said to his mother, "Mother, the big Black Dragon has become mad with anger! He won't stop the lake from flooding. The crops are inundated and the people are in a panic—they are afraid of drowning! The whole country will be devastated.

Something must be done! The big Black Dragon must be subdued!"

"Of course, but who can stand up to the big Black Dragon?" asked his worried mother.

"I can!" said her son. "I know I can, for the gods have chosen me to do battle against him."

At first his mother was mute with astonishment and terror, then she tried to hold her son back, but she knew that she could do nothing to change his destiny.

The child then announced to everyone that he was going to attack the big Black Dragon alone! Even in the midst of their panic, great astonishment overtook the people.

"He is much too young!" they said all around him. "And even if the gods are with him, he will never be able to vanquish the terrible Black Dragon!"

"I will be able to! I know I will be able to!" repeatedly insisted the little Dragon of Yun Nan.

"They say that he was born from a dragon pearl!" said some of the inhabitants of Tali to whom his mother had spoken.

"A phoenix was present at his birth!" those who had listened to his mother added very softly with admiration.

"I will conquer him," the child affirmed again, "if you will prepare for me all of the things that I will need! And I promise you that the banks of the lake will be spared and that the inhabitants and all their crops will be saved!"

"What do you wish? Speak!" the people who were crowded around him said at last. They felt so helpless that they were ready to put their confidence in a child and to bring him anything he asked for.

"First," announced the Dragon of Yun Nan, "I need a dragon's head made of yellow copper, two pairs of claws made of steel, and six very well-sharpened knives."

The people noted all that he ordered and were wide-eyed at such assurance. It seemed as if the child were guided by a supernatural will.

"I also need," he continued, "three hundred steam-baked

rolls, and three hundred balls of iron that look exactly like the steam-baked rolls. And if you will prepare for me three dragons made of straw, I promise you that I will finish off the big Black Dragon before you all perish in the waters of Lake Eul."

Immediately the people hurried to do all that the boy ordered, while the water of the lake continued to rise and the anger of the big Black Dragon threatened to drown them all. As soon as the dragon's head of yellow copper was completed, the child put it on his head. The people then brought him the claws. He put one pair on his hands and the other on his feet.

Before jumping into the water in front of the silent crowd assembled at the edge of the lake, he took one knife between his teeth and one in each hand, and asked that someone attach three more knives to his back.

Already the little boy no longer looked like a child, but more like a little yellow dragon.

"And now," he cried in a voice that was no longer the same, "throw the three straw dragons into the lake. You will see the big Black Dragon hurl himself upon them and begin to waste his strength in a useless struggle."

The three false dragons were put into the water. The big Black Dragon immediately appeared and, causing an enormous wave, began to fight them.

"When you see yellow waves coming to the surface of the lake," said the child-become-dragon, "immediately throw me the three hundred baked rolls, because that will mean that I am hungry! And when you see the water of the lake become black, throw all the iron balls in the shape of rolls to the big Black Dragon. And when at last I have defeated him, life will again become beautiful on the banks of Lake Eul! Then throw a bale of straw into the water. At the spot where the current takes it, build a temple to the little Yellow Dragon, who will never come back again to live on the banks of Lake Eul."

And the child-dragon dove into the waters of Lake Eul to fight the big Black Dragon, who had become mad with anger.

Immediately the combat began. The waves rose to several hundred meters and enormous eddies formed. The people of Tali and the neighboring countryside looked at this perplexing spectacle in terror, uttering cries to encourage the little Yellow Dragon. A few of the more courageous ones had taken their small boats and followed the battle more closely.

After a long time pieces of the three straw dragons were scattered on the surface of the lake. Soon all the spectators saw the yellow waves that the little Yellow Dragon had told them to watch for. At the same moment, there emerged from a wave the copper head of the little Yellow Dragon, his jaws wide open to show that he was hungry. Then they threw him the three hundred rolls that were to satisfy his hunger and renew his strength.

Now the water became black. The big Black Dragon in his turn showed that he was hungry by thrusting his enormous head out of a whirlpool of water. He opened his wide and terrifying jaws. Immediately, as the child had commanded, the people threw him the three hundred balls of iron in the form of baked rolls.

The Black Dragon pounced on the iron rolls. Soon he was seen twisting in pain. The balls of iron had reached his stomach! But he continued to battle furiously against the little Yellow Dragon with the copper head and steel claws.

The battle lasted three more days. At the end, no longer able to go on, the big Black Dragon opened his jaws again, hoping someone would give him something to eat. The little Yellow Dragon was waiting for this moment. Armed with his two pairs of claws and his six steel knives, he slipped into the mouth of the big Black Dragon. He passed through his horrible open jaws, arrived in his stomach, and began to stab him from the inside.

The big Black Dragon was suffering terribly, he twisted and rolled and raised huge waves of black water. Then finally, too exhausted to fight any longer, he began to ask the little Yellow Dragon for mercy. The crowd gathered on the banks of the lake and the men who were in boats could hear, "Little Yellow Dragon! Get out of my stomach quickly! I can't stand it any longer; it is unbearable! Get out! Get out! I beg of you! I am going to leave; I will go away, and I will never again come back to the waters of Lake Eul. I leave you my palace and you will rule in my place."

"Perfect. I will be delighted to leave your stomach. But how shall I get out?"

"Leave through one of my nostrils. But be quick!"

"I will never leave from there! People will think that you blew your nose to get rid of me! After my victory over you in battle, that would be ridiculous!"

"All right, then go out through my ear, if you prefer."

"Absurd! People will say that you cleaned out your ear by having me leave—I who beat you!"

"Little Yellow Dragon, leave, I beg of you! Leave from under my armpit, then."

"Certainly not! You would try to crush me."

And all this time, the little Yellow Dragon, with his two pairs of claws and his six steel knives, continued to make the big Black Dragon suffer, to punish him for having caused terror on the banks of Lake Eul, ruining the people's crops and threatening to drown them.

"Little Yellow Dragon, that's enough! Leave through my eye. I can no longer stand you inside me."

And that is what the little Yellow Dragon did. He pierced the right eye of the big Black Dragon and emerged triumphant. From that time on the big Black Dragon was one-eyed.

The defeated dragon slipped to the bottom of the lake and made a hole under the rocks so that he could escape to the sea. And he was never seen again in the waters of Lake Eul.

At once the level of the lake was lowered. The water that had already flooded its banks drained through the hole the big Black Dragon had made. This passage is now called The Arch of the Bridge of the Sky.

The little Yellow Dragon was cheered by the grateful people, but he never again came back onto the land. He rules over the waters of Lake Eul, and people say he can sometimes be seen among the waves.

A bale of straw was thrown into the lake as the child had asked before becoming the little Yellow Dragon. On the spot where the bale of straw stopped floating, they built a temple to him. The inhabitants of Tali and the land around it always honored the little Yellow Dragon as their god. Another temple was constructed for his mother alongside the temple of the Three Pagodas of Tali.

Not a single Chinese has ever forgotten the battle of the courageous little Yellow Dragon against the big Black Dragon, and each year the Feast of the Dragons is celebrated on the fifth day of the fifth lunar month before the season of the sun.

The Ox Driver and the Weaver

Among the splendors of the Heaven of the East, there lived the all-powerful Dragon King. From his magnificent palace of gold and jade, he commanded the winds and the rain. The morning dew obeyed him as did the evening fog, the storm, and the squall. Whenever he was angry, thunderbolts fell from the sky.

The Dragon King also reigned over an immense family. He had many wives, each one more beautiful than the other. He had thousands of men and women servants, and his children were as countless as the stars in the sky.

However, he knew them all, and his favorite daughter had always been the ravishing little Princess Silver Lotus. But in this sumptuous palace where all these immortal beings lived happily, the beautiful princess was bored all day long. Truly, it was worthless to be beautiful and immortal in the splendors of the Heaven of the East, because her heart was empty.

When she was not weaving gorgeous cloths of gold and silk in colors of the rising sun, Princess Silver Lotus wandered about the vast rooms of the palace, looking for someone whom she could love. But she knew she could never meet him in the Heaven of the East. So the beautiful princess went back and forth in her vast domain, looking for a way to escape.

She knew, however, that she did not have the right to cross the boundaries of the sky in order to go down to earth. Each time that she tried, a celestial guardian rose up before her in his shining armor and brought her back to her father the king.

"My daughter," cried the Dragon King, "is not the Heaven of the East big and fine enough for you? You are immortal and very beautiful, and you will find your happiness among us, or you will be punished forever — forever!"

For a long time the sentence of the Dragon King echoed across the halls of his palace. Then Silver Lotus wisely took up once more her spindles of silk in colors of the rising sun and started again to weave. Still her heart remained empty, and she knew that one day she must succeed in leaving the Heaven of the East to visit the earth.

Finally there came a great festival day — the nine-hundredth birthday of the Dragon King. Even the celestial guards were invited; the whole sky was in a state of excitement. No one would have believed that Princess Silver Lotus could choose this day to run away.

It seemed very easy to her. She called the little flossy cloud that she usually used for riding around the Heaven of the East and ordered it to take her to the land of the humans. The little cloud asked for nothing better than to travel a bit. He descended into the land of China, bringing the princess with him, and left her on the bank of Lake Qing Hai. Then he went back immediately to the Heaven of the East because he did not want to lose his place at the celebration.

The little princess was completely dumbfounded to find herself alone at the edge of a rice field. And while, perhaps with a bit of regret, she watched her cloud disappear, the delightful air of a flute came to her ears. It sang beautifully of a lovely, simple joy and already it had warmed her heart. Who could possibly play such music in these solitary parts?

Guided by the melody, Silver Lotus soon discovered an enormous ox on which was mounted a boy about her own age. The boy had not seen her and he continued to play his flute skillfully.

Around him, numerous birds of all plumages and all colors flew silently. Some blue magpies arrived at full speed and gathered in a circle around the young man. They seemed charmed by his music. Several of them even perched on the ox, others continued to fly or perched close by.

The young Princess Silver Lotus approached silently. She, too, found herself captivated by the song of the ox driver. When he noticed her, still and beautiful, before him, his flute fell from his hands. He had discovered Beauty!

The music had ceased, but Silver Lotus remained wide-eyed and quiet, completely overcome, contemplating this handsome boy, still seated on his ox. He had the gift of charming the birds and he had enchanted her, too. She had just met the companion she was seeking, the one whom she had not been able to find in the Heaven of the East, and her heart was no longer empty.

"I am Niu Lang, the ox driver," the boy said at last, getting down from his ox and holding it by its halter. "I live with my mother in that cabin by the edge of Lake Qing Hai. I tend our ox while playing the flute; that is all I know how to do."

"And I, I am Silver Lotus, one of the many daughters of the Dragon King," answered the princess, handing him his flute, which she had just picked up. "I have come from the Heaven of the East to meet you. And all I know how to do is weave!"

It was thus that Niu Lang and Princess Silver Lotus became acquainted, and they loved one another immediately.

Leading his ox by the halter, Niu Lang set out on the road towards his poor little house, taking Silver Lotus with him to introduce her to his mother. Several days later they were married.

Meanwhile, in the Heaven of the East, the festivities continued. They lasted through the entire time of the Moon. But when the celebration was over and the Dragon King became aware of the disappearance of his favorite daughter, he had a terrible fit of anger! One hundred times he sent thunderbolts down to earth. Storms, tempests, and squalls shook the country of the humans where little Silver Lotus had fled and hidden herself. However, she was not frightened into returning to the Heaven of the East.

Then the Dragon King dispatched his fifty celestial troops to earth with orders to bring the beautiful princess back to his palace in the Heaven of the East. But on the banks of Lake Qing Hai, the young ox driver, Niu Lang, who had married his extraordinary gift from heaven, seemed stronger than the Dragon King. Seated on his ox, Niu Lang continued to play the flute and to charm the birds. Coming from all the corners of the sky, the blue magpies of China gathered around him to listen to his wonderful music. They were so numerous that they formed a kind of blue cloud, which hid the two lovers from the soldiers of the Dragon King.

Since she had come to stay in the house at the edge of Lake Qing Hai, little Silver Lotus had been weaving her marvelous tapestries in the colors of the sky of the Orient. Her works brightened the walls of the poor little house, and from her labors the family lived. She was no longer called Silver Lotus, but Tche Niu, which means "the weaver."

Several years passed without the Dragon King succeeding in bringing back his favorite daughter. The ox driver's mother died peacefully, knowing that she was leaving her son and her daughter-in-law perfectly happy and well protected by the blue magpies.

In her happiness, Tche Niu, the weaver, had almost forgotten the anger of her father, the Dragon King. All her love and her care went to her husband, and her nimble fingers continued to weave beautiful tapestries.

Niu Lang did not play his flute to charm the birds as often as he used to. He now had several oxen to tend and he had enlarged his house. Little by little the magpies became less careful in their vigilance. They still formed a group around Niu Lang and Tche Niu to guard them when they went to the edge of the lake, but this was not enough to keep them safe.

When the Dragon King again sent all his celestial troops to earth, his envoys noticed the young weaver walking calmly at the edge of the lake with her husband. They surrounded her immediately and carried her away before the very eyes of Niu Lang before the magpies had time to intervene.

A large gray storm cloud brought the princess to her father, while Niu Lang remained inconsolable on earth at the edge of Lake Qing Hai.

"You did not have the right to look for your happiness on earth!" thundered the Dragon King in his fury, "and this union with a human will only bring you grief. You will remain a prisoner of the Heaven of the East forever, for I will never be able to forgive you."

So Tche Niu once again took up her weaving in the magnificent palace of her father, who had tightly closed his gates of jade and gold. But all the time she wove, she wept for her love destroyed by the anger of the Dragon King, and her sobs echoed through the immense halls of the sumptuous palace.

The king let six moons pass, thinking that the princess, distracted by the pageantry of the Heaven of the East, would soon forget her pain.

But, when the six moons had passed, the beautiful princess was still weeping, while at the edge of Lake Qing Hai the unhappy Niu Lang, completely helpless, could no longer make his flute sing. He had lost Tche Niu and, in his grief, he had forgotten his wonderful talent.

However the birds, which he had so often charmed, would not abandon him. They gathered silently around him and they waited.

In the Heaven of the East, the Dragon King let six more moons pass, but the beautiful weaver still wept for her earthly love. The Dragon King was so exasperated by her grief that he decided to exile her to a star at the edge of the Milky Way.

And so he brought Princess Silver Lotus to a bright star alongside the Celestial River so that he would no longer hear her sad cries. But just as he was about to leave her forever, he remembered that she had been his favorite daughter before she committed her unpardonable error.

"Because of my love for you, and because of my pity for your ox driver, I will have him brought to the other side of the

Milky Way," he said to her. "He will come to live on a star across from you."

"Well then, arrange it so that Niu Lang also becomes eternal!" demanded the princess from her star. "Then we can contemplate one another forever across the Celestial River of the Milky Way."

The Dragon King agreed and sent a cloud to get Niu Lang, who still awaited the return of Tche Niu to earth.

However, the blue magpies, which the ox driver had so often charmed, would not desert him. They conceived of a way to have the husband and wife meet once a year on the day of the autumnal equinox. On that day each year the birds formed a living bridge over the Celestial River with their own bright bodies so that the husband and wife could cross over and meet each other face to face.

Even today two bright stars can be seen facing each other across the Milky Way. These stars, some believe, are the homes of the Weaver and the Ox Driver. They say in China that Niu Lang and Tche Niu are the protector gods of married love. And the magpie of China has always remained the symbol of fidelity.

The Repentant Tiger of Setchouan

Poor old San-Lang lived only for her son, Liou. He was her only son and her sole support.

One day young Liou went to walk in the hills of Setchouan where his mother could not follow him. Unfortunately a tiger met him and ate him!

Instead of dying of grief as one would have feared, old San-Lang decided to take vengeance. She gathered all her strength and courage and asked for an audience with Judge Wou. She wished to bring a complaint against the tiger and have him condemned to death.

"Judge," she said to him, "this tiger deserves to be arrested, tried, and his head cut off! He has committed an abominable crime. He has taken from me what was most precious to me in the whole world—my only son, Liou. I demand that this very day an arrest warrant be placed against this tiger."

Judge Wou knew the law perfectly and had judged a great number of trials in his lifetime. But he had never encountered such a case! First he tried to explain to old San-Lang that the law could not be applied to a tiger, whatever the terrible crime of which the animal was accused.

But old San-Lang did not wish to listen to anything, to know anything, or to understand anything! She swore that she would not leave the law court before an arrest warrant was placed against the assassin.

Then, out of respect for her great age – and also to get rid of her – the judge promised to have the tiger searched out and arrested. But the old lady would not be content with this vague promise. She declared that she would not leave the premises until she could see with her own eyes that an arrest warrant had been effectively executed against the tiger.

Judge Wou, knowing no other way to put an end to this affair, called in his subordinates and asked that one of them take charge of the matter. At first not one member of the tribunal would do anything, each one thinking that the law did not apply in this case. But as the judge insisted, his employee Li Neng, who happened to be completely drunk that day, volunteered to act. His mind was not clear enough to understand what the accusation and crime were all about, but he felt very optimistic. Li Neng announced publicly that he was taking over the case, and he immediately put out an arrest warrant for the tiger. The old lady, now appeased, went away.

When Li Neng became sober, he realized that he had been crazy to take on this case! It seemed evident to him that the promise of an arrest warrant had only been made by Judge Wou to calm the old woman and make her leave the courtroom. He tried to put this troublesome case out of his mind and to forget the tiger and the old lady.

But after some time, Judge Wou called for him and asked him if he had arrested the accused. Li Neng was obliged to say no.

"What!" the judge cried out in anger, "you promised to bring this affair to a quick conclusion and you haven't done a thing! You will have to do everything you can to end this case."

The unhappy Li Neng had no idea at all how to go about his task. When he was not drunk, he was a very serious worker, and he could hardly imagine himself running through the hills looking for the tiger. Besides, this animal was cruel and dangerous, and Li Neng did not want to be devoured like the son of old San-Lang. Then the idea came to him to ask Judge Wou for authority to order all the hunters of the region to track down the tiger in the surrounding countryside. Judge Wou granted him permission.

The men scattered into the hills to hunt for the tiger. But they looked for it in vain by day and by night. The tiger never showed itself, and eventually all the disappointed hunters went home.

A month passed, and neither Li Neng nor any of the hunters had seen the tiger. Poor Li Neng could almost feel the whip that the judge was in the habit of using when his subordinates did not execute his orders! He was even afraid that he would lose his place in the court, and he simply did not know how to get himself out of this situation. The tiger seemed to have vanished into thin air!

One day Li Neng, in the depths of despair, went to the temple of Cheng Huang to pray to the gods to help him find the tiger. It appears that the tiger took advantage of the time that had passed to reflect on his crime, for he entered the temple just behind Li Neng. He had come to ask the gods for pardon.

When Li Neng turned around, he saw the tiger kneeling in front of the altar. Trembling in fear, Li Neng believed that the animal, knowing that he was responsible for the arrest warrant, was going to devour him. He waited motionless for a fatal blow of the sharp claws. But as the tiger looked at him without the slightest wickedness, calmly sitting on his tail, Li Neng started to talk to him.

"Was it you, oh tiger, who devoured Liou, the only son of old

San-Lang? And do you know that she has brought a complaint against you?"

"I know, Li Neng, and that is why I have come to turn myself over to you here in the temple of Cheng Huang."

"If you have committed this crime, let me put my belt around your neck because I am going to take you before Judge Wou."

Meekly, the tiger offered no resistance, and Li Neng led him to the tribunal.

"Did you devour the son of the old woman, San-Lang?" asked Judge Wou.

The tiger nodded his head.

"Do you regret this terrible crime?" continued the judge.

The tiger nodded his head a second time.

"Do you know that your crime is punishable by death, and the executioner should have already cut off your head?"

The tiger indicated that he knew this.

"But," continued the judge, "young Liou was the only son of a poor woman; by eating him you have deprived her of her only support. If we condemn you to death, that will not make amends for your crime and it will not change the fate of the old lady. Do you promise to make up for your crime by serving her as her son?"

The tiger nodded his head one more time.

"If you do this, tiger, your crime will be pardoned and you will keep the old woman from dying of hunger and loneliness!"

The judge ordered that the tiger be released immediately. This made old San-Lang furious. She had no confidence in the beast that had devoured her son. However, the next morning when she opened the door of her house, she was astonished to find a large piece of meat on the doorstep! It was much more than she needed. She sold three quarters of it and with the money she bought other things she needed.

From that day on, each morning old San-Lang found an offering at her door. She could eat to her heart's content every day as in the days when her son was living with her. She also continued to sell a part of what the tiger brought, which enabled her to become rich.

Soon bonds of friendship began to strengthen between the tiger and the old woman. They got along very well together, and the woman let the tiger sleep in front of her door for days on end, and spoke to him often. The tiger became quiet and calm and only hunted in order to find food for them both.

But the old woman had lost her interest in living and she died several years later. The day old San-Lang died the tiger did not bring anything to the doorstep, but went into the house, let out a long scream, and fled into the hills.

As San-Lang had become rich thanks to the tiger, she was given a sumptuous funeral, and a large crowd attended the ceremony. Suddenly, during the funeral, the tiger bounded into the middle of the crowd, terrorizing everyone! The people believed that the tiger had once again become wicked now that he had finished atoning for his crime. They fled in all directions in complete panic.

However, the tiger paid no attention to them. For a moment he lay down on the burial mound, then getting up, he let out a terrible roar and disappeared behind the hills. He was never seen again, but in his memory, the people constructed a monument next to old San-Lang's gravestone.

Qing Yang and His Winged Horse

Long, long ago, in the time when the earth was lit by the seven suns and the six moons, the hero Qing Yang was born in China on the coast of the Oriental Sea. At that time many people and many beasts already lived on earth. The Emperor of Heaven had instructed them to live in equality and peace. When Qing Yang grew up, the Emperor of Heaven put him in charge of watching over the earth.

One spring day, Qing Yang said good-bye to his two wives, who lived on two different islands in the Oriental Sea, and went off for a long voyage, mounted on his flying horse.

Qing Yang had already traveled through half the world, when he noticed at the foot of Liang Chu Mountain a multitude of all species of birds, pressed one against the other, and chirping sadly. There were larks, quail, orioles, doves, eagles, and kites. They did not fly away upon the arrival of Qing Yang, and when he spoke to them, they all lifted their heads and looked at him.

"Birds of the world," said Qing Yang, "the Emperor of Heaven desires that all the beasts of the earth live happily and peacefully together. Why then are you so sad?"

"Once we were happy, sir, but we have been miserable for a long time now," answered a lark with a pure voice. "Zhao the Python, who resembles a demon, demands the tribute of one bird per day. He will end up by killing all the birds of the world!"

"But why don't you all make war on him with blows of your beaks, claws, and wings? Then you can have peace once more," said Qing Yang.

The birds all began to speak at once, making a terrible noise, "Declare war on Zhao the Python? We would never be able to do that, never! The light of the six moons has given him a giant, powerful body, and the heat of the seven suns has given him incomparable strength!"

"No one can do anything against him!" added the lark. "Indeed, who would be able to vanquish the seven suns and the six moons, which have made a veritable monster of Zhao?"

"Very well, then, I am going to take care of this matter!" said the hero Qing Yang. He mounted his winged steed, Zhou Kai, which in a few seconds brought him to Mount Liang.

When he arrived at the top of the mountain that almost touched the sky, Qing Yang took his bow, drew it, and aimed an arrow at one of the seven suns.

The sun, hit by the arrow, was immediately changed into a ball of black smoke, which fell into the sea. Now there remained only six suns! Qing Yang took another arrow, drew his bow, and aimed. The second sun fell into the sea. And in the same way, the third, the fourth, then the fifth and the sixth, all fell in black smoke into the sea!

But when the hero Qing Yang wanted to aim at the seventh sun, it began to talk to him from high in the sky. "Stop, Qing Yang! Stop! If you hit me, all warmth will disappear from the earth forever. All the creatures of the earth will die of cold and you will too!"

"You are right," cried Qing Yang, "I will not make you fall into the sea, but you must never again give warmth to evil-doing creatures!"

The birds, who had seen the six suns fall, chirped for joy, "We are saved! The monster Zhao is going to die of cold!"

"But he will only cease to be dangerous," cried the kite, "when the moons will also have fallen!"

Qing Yang waited for night to fall, then he took an arrow from his quiver and aimed at the first moon. At once the moon fell behind the mountain. And as Qing Yang shot his arrows, the second, third, fourth, and fifth moons fell one after the other behind Mount Liang. But when he wanted to aim at the sixth one, it cried out from high in the sky, "Stop, Qing Yang! Stop! If you make me fall, the earth will lose its light forever. All the creatures will be blind, and so will you!"

"Very well, you are right," Qing Yang answered. "I will not make you fall behind the mountain, but you must no longer light the way for evil creatures!"

All the birds, pressed close against one another, had watched the six suns fall into the sea and the five moons disappear behind the mountain. Now they sang for joy. They came from everywhere to see the hero, Qing Yang, who had come down from the mountain. The hero dragged behind him the python, which had returned to its normal size and was no longer dangerous.

It seemed to Qing Yang that all the birds of the earth were there, flying in a great circle around him. Qing Yang was deafened by their joyous cries and dazzled by the colors of their plumage.

"We thank you, Qing Yang!" said all the birds at once.

"Zhao the Python is no longer a demon. Peace has returned to us!"

"Be happy forever as the Emperor of Heaven wishes you to be!" answered the hero, as he flew away on his winged steed to continue his voyage around the world.

Some time later, Qing Yang dismounted at the entrance of a village near Mount Da Mao. It seemed to him that a great misfortune threatened this country. All the inhabitants walked with lowered heads, tormented glances, and worried looks. He stopped an old woman who was passing by and asked her, "Can you tell me what unhappiness weighs so heavily on this land? Why do you not all live together in peace as the Emperor of Heaven wishes?"

"Once we were happy, but that was long ago," answered the woman. "A frightful monster lives in Lake Po Yang. At first he just attacked our herds from time to time. Then he began to come every day to devour our steers and cows and lambs. Then he commanded us to bring a new victim to him at the edge of the lake every day. We no longer have any steers or cows. We have only a single lamb left in the village! The grass is growing everywhere with no animals to eat it. The water of the spring flows uselessly with no animals to drink it. And now that we no longer have any beasts to give to the monster, he is going to ask for people!"

"The will of the Emperor of Heaven is that men and beasts shall live on the earth in peace. I will let no one disturb that peace!" Qing Yang said furiously. "What do you know of this monster?"

"We have never seen him, but the sorcerer of Mount Da Mao says that it is a monstrous dragon," answered the terrorized villagers gathered around Qing Yang.

Immediately, the hero remounted his winged horse and went to see the sorcerer of Mount Da Mao.

"Sorcerer!" he said severely, "what are you doing to destroy this bloodthirsty monster?"

"I have said so many prayers that my lips are worn out!" answered the sorcerer hanging his head.

"This dragon cannot be appeased by your prayers! But is it possible to harm him in the water of the lake?" asked the hero.

"Impossible," answered the sorcerer, "and even on the banks of the lake, a steel sword nine times tempered cannot wound him."

"Have you tried fire?" asked the hero.

"No," admitted the sorcerer, "but how could we burn him?"

"I can take care of that!" answered Qing Yang as he jumped on his winged horse and flew away toward the east.

The hero soon came to a high mountain that was completely black and barren. It was called the Mountain of Fire. Qing Yang went around the mountain three times, gathered up three solid bars of iron, and returned to the village on his flying steed. He made this round trip in less time than it takes to eat a bowl of rice!

Qing Yang asked all the inhabitants of the village to gather up firewood. Then he lit an enormous fire on the banks of the lake in order to make the three bars of iron white hot.

There was only one lamb left in the village and Qing Yang had it slaughtered. Then he placed it under the three iron bars, which had been arranged in the form of a portico.

The lamb began to roast, heated by the iron bars, and it smelled delicious. The wind soon carried this appetizing scent towards Lake Po Yang, just as Qing Yang had expected it would.

Suddenly an enormous wave raised the waters of the lake. With a terrible roar, a monstrous black dragon with red eyes came out of the water, claws first, and bounded towards the lamb. He had barely put his teeth into the roasted lamb, when the red-hot iron bars fell in on him. The dragon, caught in this fiery trap, struggled with all his might, roaring dreadfully, but he could not free himself. He died of his burns on the edge of Lake Po Yang.

All the inhabitants of the village came out of their houses to see the dead dragon, and they all began to talk of Qing Yang with gratitude. The men admired his intelligence and his courage, and the women repeated to their children, "Never forget what you have just seen — the death of this monstrous black dragon and the bravery of our hero, Qing Yang! You will still remember it when you are old and we are no longer here!"

The hero mounted his winged horse and then spoke to the grateful crowd.

"The will of the Emperor of Heaven is that all his creatures live in peace on earth. No one has the right to disturb this peace. The python lost its power, the ferocious and bloodthirsty dragon is dead! Let no one live by oppressing others!"

Soon Qing Yang was only a tiny dot on the horizon while the villagers still danced for joy.

After leaving the country, Qing Yang went directly to his first wife, who waited for him on an island in the Oriental Sea. Seeing him come back after so long an absence, she cried for joy, then she listened to him tell of his extraordinary feats and she praised him greatly.

But this woman now wanted to have Qing Yang for herself alone. She wanted to keep him from departing again, for the peace of the world was less important to her than her own happiness. During the night, she got up without a sound and went secretly to the stable to cut a wing off her husband's flying horse.

Before dawn the next day, Qing Yang decided to visit his second wife on another island in the Oriental Sea. He got up and left his house without waking his first wife. He took his steed from the stable, but he did not notice the missing wing. He mounted into the saddle, and the horse rose into the air. However, it had to make a tremendous effort to carry its master to his destination.

The second wife of Qing Yang also cried for joy on seeing him return after such a long absence. Then she listened as her husband told her how he had rendered Zhao the Python harmless and killed the monstrous black dragon that had troubled the peace of the inhabitants of the earth. She showed Qing Yang her greatest admiration.

However, this woman also wished to have Qing Yang to herself and to prevent him from leaving again; for the peace of the world was far less important to her than her own happiness. While her husband was sleeping, she went to the stable and cut off the second wing of Qing Yang's magnificent flying charger.

The hero knew that he must leave once more to travel the earth and bring peace to the places where peace did not reign. He got up even earlier than the night before, went silently out into the moonless night, and took his horse from the stable.

Once his master was in the saddle the great horse bounded into the air as he had always done. But without his wings he could not fly through the sky!

The horse tumbled several times in space, neighing painfully. Even before the second wife, who had run up to the water's edge, had time to cry out, Qing Yang and his wingless horse were snatched up by the sea. "Qing Yang is at the bottom of the sea! Qing Yang is at the bottom of the sea!" cried the wife.

Immediately the news spread far and wide over the earth, causing immense sorrow among all the peoples and beasts of the world.

Since that time, when birds fly over the Oriental Sea, they utter harsh, sad cries. They are calling for the body of Qing Yang, which the waves will never return to them. The waves of the Oriental Sea continue to moan. It is the only answer that the sea has ever given.

Lien Houa, the Pretentious Turtle

There were three friends who lived at the edge of the little Lake of Tranquility—Tching and Tchang the two herons, and Lien Houa, the turtle whose name meant "Lotus Flower."

The two herons never told Lien Houa that she was slow or cumbersome or not very elegant, and the turtle, content with her lot, believed herself to be beautiful and even intelligent. She never thought of envying the elegance of her two friends, who knew how to fish with the end of their beaks, run lightly over the sandbank, and fly gracefully into the sky.

Tching, Tchang, and Lien Houa played on the beach, strutting along in the sun, sharing their catch of fish, without a care in the world!

Unfortunately, there came a period of terrible drought. In this particular year, not a single drop of rain fell from the second to the eighth month. The beds of all the rivers and lakes could be seen through the shallow water, the cotton and the rice fields were dried out, and the water level of the little Lake of Tranquility began to get very low. The lake was disappearing before their very eyes and the three friends became more and more troubled.

What was to become of the three inseparables? For Tching and Tchang there was no problem. They could fly as far as the ocean if it were necessary. But the turtle got around so slowly that she would be dead of thirst ten times over before arriving at the slightest puddle of water!

One day, the two herons came to announce to Lien Houa that it was absolutely necessary to move immediately if they did not all wish to die on the spot of hunger and thirst.

They had already waited much too long! All of the other inhabitants of the region had left a long time ago and had headed towards Lake Celeste. They had all moved, even the moles and the lizards. No one was left.

"And how about me?" Lotus Flower started to weep and cry out. "You know very well that I will never be able to follow you on such a long voyage dragging my shell. Are you, then, going to abandon me?"

The herons, perched on one foot, were really upset. They did not know what to say to Lien Houa, who continued to reproach them. "Leave, go ahead, leave! False friends that you are! And let me die here alone of sadness and thirst under my shell! Ah, what a misfortune to have believed in one's friends!"

On seeing her cry like that, Tching and Tchang each shed several tears, but it wasn't enough to make the level of the lake rise. They decided to wait a little while longer. Maybe it would finally rain tomorrow or the next day.

But the third day it still had not rained and the Lake of Tranquility was almost completely dry!

Seeing the two herons consulting together, and knowing that today she could no longer detain them by crying and weeping, Lien Houa said to them, "Why do you not find a way to take me with you? You know that you will miss me very much if I do not come with you."

But she, who thought herself to be so intelligent, could not find the solution. It was Tching and Tchang who suggested to her, "We can fly away taking you with us, Lian Houa. All we need to do is find a good strong stick! We will each take an end in our beaks, and you will bite it in the middle so we can carry you through the air!"

"Marvelous! Magnificent! Sublime! Celestial!" cried the turtle, trying to jump for joy. "See, I was right to tell you to find a way to take me with you! Ah, I am the one who must always think of everything! Come on! Go find a stick and let's leave right away! I have had enough of this unbearable drought!"

The two herons found a good stout stick and warned Lien Houa several times not to forget to keep her mouth closed very tightly on the stick throughout the voyage. They were going to fly at a high altitude and great speed. If she let go of the stick, they would lose her forever!

The turtle puffed herself up, thinking that they really cared a great deal for her.

"Count on me!" she said to them, "and fly as high and as fast as you wish! Nothing will make me open my mouth; I'm not that stupid!"

Thus Lotus Flower flew away carried by Tching and Tchang. Very happy with her lot, forgetting for a while the weight of her shell, Lien Houa let herself be carried while biting solidly on the stick.

The two herons flew on towards Lake Celeste. The turtle saw immense forests of bamboo, long rice fields, vast plains, and sparkling mountains covered with snow as they passed beneath her. What a journey! Never would Lien Houa have believed that the earth was so large.

Still Tching and Tchang flew on and on. Lien Houa saw palaces, temples, and pagodas with golden roofs go by. Several times while passing over a village, she saw the peasants raise their heads and point their fingers in admiration. She even heard the villagers say, "Oh! Look! See how intelligent that turtle is! She has found a way to travel without getting tired! She is having herself transported by two herons! What a good idea!"

Tching and Tchang continued to fly conscientiously. They did not even hear what was being said below. As for the turtle, her heart jumped for joy, for nothing pleased her as much as feeling that she was admired.

While the two herons were flying above a vast prairie, Lien Houa saw two little shepherds excitedly pointing their fingers at her. The turtle, hoping to hear new compliments, lent an ear.

"See what is happening in the sky!" exclaimed the shepherds. "Two herons are carrying a turtle. How intelligent those herons are! They have finally found a way to make that stupid turtle travel! At least they don't have to wait for her!"

The herons did not pay any attention to this remark. They wanted to arrive at Lake Celeste as soon as possible and they only thought about flying.

But the turtle was very angry. "What imbeciles!" she said to herself. "What nerve to talk without knowing the truth!" For actually, if Tching and Tchang had not found this ingenious means of transportation, she would have proposed it to them. She was not, after all, more stupid than they!

In her anger, she opened her mouth to explain to them, "Hey, you dummies!"

And PLOP!

They never knew that it was she who was the most intelligent, for Lien Houa took an immense dive from high in the sky into a little pond of frozen water, which quickly cooled the flames of her anger.

Alas! It was too late when the two herons, always busily flying towards Lake Celeste, noticed that they had lost Lien Houa in flight.

And it is thus that Lien Houa, the stupid turtle, incapable of traveling alone to Lake Celeste, finished her days in a little pond among the lotus flowers, who never believed in her extraordinary voyage and thought her a terrible show-off!

For the Love of Yu Houa

Pure as a diamond, precious as pearl and jade, Yu Houa had married Che Touen at the springtime festival. In addition to her ravishing beauty, Yu Houa possessed all the virtues. Her husband, Che Touen, was a good–hearted young man, intelligent and industrious. The couple adored each other; they were made for happiness.

Unfortunately, they both lived in the home of Che Touen's mother, who was so jealous of her daughter-in-law that she made her life unbearable. This miserable woman had but one goal—to make Yu Houa unhappy. Each day she went out of her way to criticize Yu Houa. She was not happy with the delicious dishes her daughter-in-law prepared and she did not

hesitate to invent ugly lies, pretenses for new reproaches. She even went so far as to beat poor Yu Houa.

Che Touen despaired when he saw his wife, whom he knew to be faultless, suffer so. Alas! Tradition forbade him to interfere. He watched miserably as pretty Yu Houa lost her gaiety and her freshness.

One evening, returning to his mother's home, Che Touen found Yu Houa completely discouraged.

"Dear Che Touen!" she said to him, tears running down her face, "I have already suffered too much, I cannot go on! I would like to die, but I love you too much to want to leave you like this!"

"Yu Houa! I see that you can no longer stand all the wickedness my mother has inflicted on you. Tonight as soon as the moon rises, we will flee to another country."

On hearing these words Yu Houa's face lit up with joy. "Is it possible, dear Che Touen," she said, "that we can leave this house forever?"

"Our love will be stronger than the hate that wishes to destroy it. We will leave together as soon as night comes!"

Towards midnight, Che Touen and Yu Houa left the house without a sound, empty-handed. They carried with them only their love and their hope. They untied two thin horses from the stable and left the village without awakening a soul.

Their way lighted by the moon, Che Touen and Yu Houa fled at a great speed, as if their poor mounts wished to save them from a terrible misfortune. From village to village they rode. And they soon arrived at the foot of a high mountain. They no longer had any idea where they were, but Che Touen did not pause.

"Forward!" he said to the horses, who seemed tireless in spite of their feeble appearance. The faithful steeds threw themselves forward, making the stones roll under their hooves.

At daybreak they arrived at a sort of high plateau covered with green grass. It was springtime, the apple trees and the apricot trees were in bloom, birds were singing in the bushes, cranes were flying in the blue sky. Yu Houa sighed deeply and said to Che Touen, "The birds have their nests—they are happy—but we, what is to become of us on this unknown mountain? Where will we find a home?"

"All we need is a little shelter of leaves under which to spend the night, dear Yu Houa," answered her husband. "Why worry when you are with me?"

Then Yu Houa forgot her sadness and said to him, "It's true, Che Touen, all I ask is to spend the rest of my life with you!"

Soon they started off in the saddle again, scaled rocky slopes, crossed ravines, and descended the other side of the mountain.

Then all of a sudden their horses stopped in front of an extraordinary spring. The water of this spring was red and transparent. It shimmered in the sun and its reflection made the grass, the leaves, the flowers, and all that surrounded it glow red.

When Yu Houa got down from her horse and drew near, she seemed to breathe a delicious perfume. Was it the water of this stream that perfumed the air? Or the red flowers that scented it? Yu Houa wanted to stop a moment at this place.

"We are tired, Che Touen," she said. "The horses are tired too. Please let us rest a moment near this red spring."

Che Touen dismounted. The tired couple let their horses graze, and they approached the red spring. The water sparkled, it was as clear as crystal! Yu Houa realized that she was very thirsty. She knelt down, scooped up some water in her cupped hands, and took a long sip.

"It is as sweet as honey, fresher than the dew!" she said to her husband. "Aren't you coming to drink, too?"

At that very moment she felt a strange softness through her whole body. When she raised her head Che Touen, who was watching her drink, noticed that all signs of fatigue were gone from her face, which was shining with beauty. Her skin had taken on the glow of a peach blossom and her eyes glistened.

At the same time the horses, who had also come to drink at the red spring, neighed joyously. The two young people turned around to look at them and were astounded by their transformation! Their coats seemed more lustrous, their flanks appeared less thin — the animals had become magnificent!

Fear suddenly invaded the hearts of Yu Houa and Che Touen. They could not understand what had taken place at the edge of that mysterious red spring. Perhaps the spring was bewitched! They hastily remounted their horses and left at a gallop.

The horses ran faster than before. They climbed the slopes of the mountains as easily as they had earlier galloped over flat terrain. They jumped streams, bounded across ravines, and ran day and night without stopping or tiring.

When Che Touen and Yu Houa finally dared look back, the mountain at the foot of which was the red spring was now only a bluish spot on the horizon. They slowed their horses because they were coming to a small village.

The first house they came to was lit up, and Yu Houa and Che Touen knocked at the door to ask for shelter. The old lady who immediately came to open the door for them, looked at them with astonishment.

"You are not from around here, that is clear!" she said to them. "Perhaps I can help you?"

Yu Houa felt herself attracted to the kindly old woman, and the warmth of this house did her good.

"Indeed we have come very far," she said, "and we haven't met anyone for three days, and soon it will be three nights. Could we stay with you, grandmother?"

The old lady was delighted and opened her door wide and said to them, "Certainly! I have a lovely room for the two of you. You will sleep better here than at the inn."

After their long ride, Che Touen and Yu Houa found the warm welcome of the old lady very good. They joyously accepted her invitation to stay with her. The old lady immediately started to prepare a good meal of rice and fish for them.

The young couple were not afraid to tell her why they had left their faraway country. They told the old lady about their entire voyage and spoke to her of the red spring at which Yu Houa had drunk.

Then the old lady began to wail and weep.

"My children," she cried, "my poor children! You will not be able to stay here together for long. A misfortune will soon separate you!"

As Che Touen and Yu Houa, completely stunned, did not understand what she meant, she started to explain to them. "The water of the red spring from which Yu Houa drank comes from the Red Mountain where the great red maple grows. The water of the spring issues from the roots of this tree. Each year in the autumn, at the time when the leaves of the maple start to turn red, the maple is no longer a tree, but becomes a horrible demon with a red face and piercing eyes that see across mountains and through rocks! He is there at the top of the Red Mountain and he watches the women who come to drink the water of the red spring. He waits for the most beautiful one, and after a while he comes for her and carries her away to make her his wife. She is never seen again! After autumn passes, at the time of the first snows, the demon with a red face again becomes a maple tree, and so does his new wife."

Yu Houa, with anguish in her heart, tried to reassure the old lady while reassuring herself.

"Grandmother," she said to her, "the demon with the red face won't carry me away. I love Che Touen too much to let that happen to me!"

And Che Touen, without wishing to show his anxiety, added, "No demon can separate us, because our love will forever be stronger than any demon!"

The old lady dried her tears, stopped her wailing, and said, "I am alone; you seem to be good children, stay then in my house since you no longer have one of your own. We will live as a family, the three of us."

She also thought that she could watch over them and perhaps chase the demon with the red face when he came to look for Yu Houa.

Che Touen and Yu Houa were happy to stay with the good old woman. From that day on the two young people shared the work of the house and the fields. The old woman had only to rest and eat the delicious meals that the charming Yu Houa prepared for her. All three were perfectly happy.

The days passed. Che Touen had gathered in the wheat, the fruits were ripening, and the trees were beginning to turn red.

Autumn had arrived and the old woman no longer could think of anything but the red leaves of the maple trees. She did not want to let the lovely Yu Houa out of her sight and she followed her everywhere. She counted on her fingers the number of days that remained before the autumnal equinox. How she wished that autumn was already over!

One day, the old woman was in the courtyard when Che Touen was returning from the fields. She heard the pure voice of Yu Houa, who was singing as she came back from the threshing floor. At that moment a whirlwind brought a large red maple leaf tumbling down from the sky. When the leaf touched the ground, there appeared a demon with a red face and red eyes and hair, in a huge red robe with sleeves hanging to the ground!

"Yu Houa, run for your life!" cried the terrified old woman. But it was already too late. With a sweep of his sleeve the demon made a couch appear, which carried Yu Houa up into a whirlwind of maple leaves.

When Che Touen raised his head, he could no longer see Yu Houa, but he heard in the distance the voice of the demon calling back, "Yu Houa drank the water of my red spring. She no longer is yours, now she belongs to me."

Che Touen went back into the house with the poor old woman, who was crying. His heart was broken.

"Grandmother," he said, "I must leave immediately. I promise that I will find her."

"It is useless, my child. It's not worth leaving. You are going to risk your life and you will never find Yu Houa! The demon with the red face will not return her to you. He has never returned the girls whom he carried off, and each year he carries off the most beautiful one of all!"

"I will go anyway, grandmother, because I cannot live without Yu Houa."

"Well then, since you are decided, do not leave empty-handed. At least take this sword, it will serve you well!"

Che Touen took the sword and left immediately for the Red Mountain. He was so impatient that he cried to his horse, "Horse, jump over this valley to find Yu Houa!" And the horse leapt over the valley to catch the demon.

"Horse, jump to the top of this mountain!" And the horse in a few fantastic leaps reached the summit of the mountain.

But Che Touen did not know where to begin to look for the demon and he did not see his dear Yu Houa anywhere.

"Horse," he said finally, "I want to find Yu Houa even if I have to look for her across all the mountains of China. Now take me to the top of the highest mountain! From there we will be able to look over the whole country and we will surely see her."

The horse immediately started off at a gallop. They jumped the streams, bounded over the rivers and the ravines, climbed the steepest slopes, and descended into the bottom of the valleys before again scaling other mountains. Che Touen did not hold back on the reins. He crossed from mountain to mountain without taking any rest. There was always a higher mountain in view and the horse and its rider scaled each one!

The demon had actually hidden Yu Houa in his cave in the side of the highest mountain of all. Yu Houa was there seated on a bed covered with draperies of silk. On the walls were hung magnificent tapestries.

"Forget Che Touen, now!" the demon repeated over and over. "Forget him for you will never see him again. Even if he had three heads, six arms, six legs, a magnificent horse, and an army with him, he would never be able to get here!"

But Yu Houa knew that at that very moment Che Touen was looking for her and weeping for her. Suddenly raising her head, she said, "I have drunk the water of your red spring but I will not be your wife."

A devilish laugh was his reply and the demon shouted at her, "If Che Touen can manage to get here, I will let you leave with him!"

The demon looked outside with his piercing eyes that could see through rocks. To his great surprise he saw Che Touen jump across five more mountains and come toward the cave at a gallop. Quickly the demon took off his embroidered belt and snapped it in the air. Immediately the belt changed into an enormous tiger that bounded out of the cave.

Che Touen and his horse, rushing forward at full speed, did not have time to stop—the tiger opened its enormous jaws and swallowed them both.

The demon, who was watching, chuckled again and announced to Yu Houa that the tiger was at that very moment digesting Che Touen and his horse. But Yu Houa did not listen to him, she still believed that Che Touen was going to come for her.

Inside the tiger it was as hot as a furnace. Che Touen gritted his teeth to forget his suffering, and took out the sword that the old woman had entrusted to him. With one blow he sliced open the stomach of the tiger and went out still on horseback! In place of the dead tiger there remained only an embroidered belt. At that moment, Che Touen realized that he was finally on the highest mountain and that this mountain was surely the Red Mountain of the demon with the red face.

"Horse," he said again, "I want to find Yu Houa! Help me!" And the horse ran straight in the direction of the demon's cave.

But the demon with a flick of his great sleeve touched the beautiful Yu Houa, who then became like a statue made of stone, unable to move. The demon then gave a sweep of his sleeve to each of the two silk cushions that encircled Yu Houa and they immediately became two other Yu Houas exactly the same as the real one.

Then the demon with the red face disappeared.

At this moment, Che Touen, still on horseback, arrived at the entrance of the cave. He found the door, which was encrusted with mother of pearl and jade. Che Touen dismounted and entered the great cave.

Then he stopped, dumbfounded — three Yu Houas awaited him seated on draperies of silk! All three looked at him, motionless and mute.

Che Touen could not tell which was the real Yu Houa — all three had the same skin, as fresh as a peach, the same large sad eyes, shadowed by long eyelashes. He uttered a sigh, and said, "Yu Houa! I have climbed one hundred and twenty mountains to find you, I with my horse escaped from the stomach of the tiger to come look for you—and you, you do not come toward me?"

Yu Houa heard what Che Touen was saying, but she could neither speak nor move. Her tongue remained as heavy as a millstone, her legs lifeless as rocks. Her body could not move, but her heart yearned for Che Touen and her pain was so great that tears streamed down her face.

Then Che Touen recognized which of the three was his wife. He threw himself at her, kissed her, took her up in his arms, and went running out of the cave with her.

But Yu Houa's body was still as rigid, as hard and as heavy as a statue of stone. Che Touen could not put her on the back of his horse. He kept his beloved in his arms and began to descend the side of the Red Mountain through the great forest of maples.

Yu Houa did not cry because she had spilled all her tears since the red-faced demon had carried her away. She spoke to herself, but Che Touen could not hear her.

"Dear Che Touen," she said, "put me down on the ground, you are troubling yourself too much for me. There are so many mountains to climb and descend, so many ravines to find your way through, and so many streams and rivers to cross! How will you ever get back to our old grandmother's house! Put me down on the ground!" And Yu Houa's heart was consumed with love for her husband, but she could not tell him how much she loved him.

Che Touen said to her, "Dear Yu Houa, even if you were truly transformed into a statue forever, I would not abandon you."

Suddenly, as Che Touen continued his journey through the forest of maples, a whirlwind of red leaves barred the way. His horse reared up on its hind legs neighing violently, and the red-faced demon appeared in front of them.

"Young man," he said to Che Touen, "don't go for your sword to kill me because you could not make me die. My heart is harder than stone or iron, and I have never bowed before anyone; but today because of you, I recognize that I am vanquished. Your love is stronger than I am. And I will never again try to separate a wife from her husband."

At that very moment he became a great maple in the forest of the Red Mountain. Several drops of dew rolled like pearls along the edge of its leaves and fell on the motionless body of Yu Houa.

Immediately the young woman regained her speech and movement, and she and Che Touen got on the horse that was waiting for them.

"Horse, jump over the mountains, so that we may quickly be back again at the home of our old grandmother!" they said, as they started off at a gallop.

Before the first snow, they were back at the house where the old woman waited for them. They had a beautiful long life and were the most happy of couples.

One can still see the red spring at the foot of the mountain. The women always drink from it to become more beautiful. But when the leaves of the maples turn red, the great maple no longer changes into the red-faced demon, and not one young girl has ever again been snatched away!

The Boy Who Loved Dragons

In the time when many dragons still lived in the sky and in the waters of China, Ye Gong was born.

When he realized that he was just a boy, Ye Gong regretted that he was not a dragon. How he would love to have the fabulous body of a dragon with the mind of a man!

Each time that he went to the temple with his parents, Ye Gong asked the gods to turn him into a dragon. But the gods didn't seem to hear him, because little Ye Gong grew like all children and never did become a dragon. Besides, he never even saw a dragon although he often begged heaven to send him one. All the dragons of China remained as invisible as ever.

The years went by and Ye Gong became a young man. But he still loved dragons and never stopped dreaming of becoming one himself. However, because Ye Gong still was not able to meet any real dragons, he became bored and lonely. That is why he thought of a way to surround himself with make-believe dragons.

He ordered a famous painter who had a remarkable talent for drawing extraordinary animals to come to his house, and said to him, "Wherever I lay my eyes I want to see dragons of all sizes and all shapes! I want them on the walls, the partitions, and even on the floors and ceilings of my house!"

Ye Gong was rich. The painter knew he was going to earn a great deal of money by doing what he was asked. So he covered every inch of Ye Gong's house with painted dragons. There was not a single space without a dragon! And all the dragons he painted were so real in color and form that they were truly impressive. Wherever he went in his house, Ye Gong saw dragons around him. It was exactly what he wanted, but he was not yet satisfied.

Ye Gong paid the painter, thanked him, and ordered a sculptor to come to him. This artist of great renown was the creator of the two golden dragons that guarded the entrance of the emperor's palace.

"You see these columns that support the roof of my house," Ye Gong said to him, "I want you to transform them into dragons! Take all the time you need, I will pay you accordingly, but they must be as striking as real ones!"

The artist undertook the task, which lasted for months. He made an absolutely frightening dragon of each pillar. It was exactly what Ye Gong asked of him, but Ye Gong was not yet satisfied. He paid the great sculptor, and ordered a weaver and his helpers to come.

"I want you to make," Ye Gong said to them, "six wall hangings of silk and six rugs of wool, representing black, red, and yellow dragons. I will pay you amply if your works are as lifelike as I hope!"

The weavers got busy at once. They needed several years to weave exactly what Ye Gong had ordered. When they had finished Ye Gong paid them and thought that at last he was going to be happy, surrounded by all his marvelous make-believe dragons.

But Ye Gong was not yet happy. He felt lonely, terribly lonely, in spite of the hundreds of false dragons that surrounded him!

Then one day the Grand Dragon of the sky and waters of China heard about Ye Gong and his great love of dragons and decided to appear on earth to visit him. He found out that Ye Gong was surrounded by hundreds of dragons that he had ordered painted, sculpted, and woven. The Grand Dragon was very curious about all these make-believe dragons.

One evening, without warning, the Grand Dragon knocked on the half-opened window of Ye Gong's house and without waiting for him to answer, stuck his head in!

When Ye Gong suddenly saw before him the horrible, enormous face of the real Grand Dragon, he was so frightened that he fled through the door very quickly and ran away, leaving the Grand Dragon quite alone facing all the make-believe dragons.

"What!" screamed the Grand Dragon, angrily. "This Ye Gong calls himself the friend of dragons and he flees at my arrival!"

And, in his fury, he tore all the dragons of wood, stone, bronze, wool, and silk into pieces.

When Ye Gong returned, he was cured forever of his love for dragons and well rid of all the false dragons with which he had wished to surround himself. He was, at last, very happy to be a man.

The Color of Lake Tienn

A long time ago, old Li Hao lived with her son, Li Yuan, at the edge of Lake Tienn. Li Hao, having become too old to work, busied herself in preparing rice for the meals, repairing the mats, and mending her son's tunics.

Li Yuan was a courageous and intelligent young boy. He worked without complaining from sunrise to sunset, from one end of the year to the other. However, the little family remained very poor, and often hunger and cold were felt under their roof.

So much work for so little money! Li Yuan felt that this was not right. He decided to speak about it to the god of the West, who, it was said, always answered those who went to him with their questions. Li Yuan would ask him the two questions that had tormented him since his childhood — Why did the water of Lake Tienn always remain dark when the sky was so clear? And why did his work bring neither happiness nor prosperity to his house?

Li Yuan's decision was made. He would leave at the beginning of the next moon. There was just enough time to prepare the dried fish and harvest the rice that his mother would need during his absence. He chopped enough wood to warm the house and cook the meals even if he had to be gone several seasons.

So on the night of the last moon, Li Yuan said his farewell to his mother, who knew his plans and did not try to hold him back. Thus Li Yuan left in search of the god of the West.

Li Yuan knew that he had to head toward the Country of the West and that the journey would be long and hard. But he was a brave boy and he even enjoyed the adventure. He certainly enjoyed it more than toiling on the land, which each day took all his strength without giving him happiness or prosperity in return.

Li Yuan walked forty-eight days in the direction of the Mountains of the West, stopping only to sleep in the fields and to eat the little millet cakes that his mother had prepared for him. On the forty-ninth evening, his tongue and lips were so dried out, and his back so tired, that he knocked at the door of a house to ask for a glass of water for he had not come upon a single stream since morning.

A woman opened the door and invited him to enter. She asked him to sit down in front of a low table, and hurried to serve him a bowl of rice and to bring him a pitcher of milk. When his hunger and thirst had been satisfied, she questioned him with interest.

"Young man, you are not a salesman, for you have nothing to sell me and those who pass this way are not in such a hurry as you are. You do not seem like a beggar—those who knock at my door are more demanding than you. Can you tell me the purpose of your journey?"

"Since you wish to know, I will tell you that I am going even further away. I am going up to the Heaven of the West to question the god of the West! I must know, for my mother's sake and mine, why the water of Lake Tienn is always dark even when the sky is clear, and why I must work every day of my life and still remain as poor as ever," answerd Li Yuan.

"You are right, young man! No one except the god of the West would know how to answer you. But who will give you enough strength to get to the Heaven of the West?" worried the woman.

"The strength is inside me and I know that I must see the god!" cried the young man, getting up to take his leave.

"Young man," the woman asked him, "when you see the god of the West, would you ask him a question for me?"

"I will," answered the young man. "What do you wish to know?"

"I have a daughter who is now eighteen years old," said the woman. "She is as intelligent as she is beautiful, but she never learned how to speak! Ask the god why she has not received the gift of speech."

"I promise you that I will ask him," answered Li Yuan.

The woman then gave him some little rolls and some very dry little cakes to take with him. Li Yuan courageously took up again his long journey towards the west, only stopping for a few hours a night to sleep. Thus he traveled for forty-eight days more.

The evening of the forty-ninth day he was indeed very tired! Again he knocked at the door of a house to ask for hospitality. It seemed to him that to spend a good night stretched out on a bed in the shelter of a house would renew his strength.

The old man who opened the door for him seemed to be very friendly. He prepared a meal of fried fish for him, brought him some water with which to wash himself, and offered him a bed. Then, in his turn, he wanted to know where the voyager was going.

"Young man, you do not speak like the people who live in these parts, and your boots are almost worn out. It seems to me that you have come from a far country," he said.

"I come from the shores of Lake Tienn and I must leave again tomorrow morning," answered Li Yuan.

"Stay with me several days to rest yourself. What is it that is so urgent?"

"I am going to the Heaven of the West to question the god! And I do not want to make my mother wait any longer. I must know for her sake and for my own why the water of Lake Tienn is always dark even when the sky is clear, and why I must work every day of my life and still remain as poor as ever!" answered Li Yuan.

"You have good reasons to go there, young man," said the old man, "and you are very brave to make such a voyage. When you come face to face with the god of the West, would you ask him a question for me?"

"I will," answered the young man. "What do you want to know?"

"My orchard is full of orange trees," explained the old man. "I planted them myself more than fifty years ago, and I take care of them every day. Never have they given me a single fruit! I would like to know why."

"I promise you that I will ask him about it," answered Li Yuan, without hesitation.

He spent the night with the old man and as soon as dawn came, he set out on his journey again. The old man had filled his bag with soy cakes, and Li Yuan once again made the food last for forty-nine days, and he drank only the water from springs and streams.

On the evening of the forty-ninth day, Li Yuan came to the banks of a wide river with turbulent waters. He was very, very tired. Not seeing any ferryman, the boy sat down on a big rock and anxiously asked himself how he was going to cross these deep waters.

Suddenly thunder rumbled and the whole countryside became dark. A violent wind arose and swept over the yellow water of the river. On the highest wave there appeared a magnificent dragon whose scales were as green as jade. At the same time a rainbow suddenly shone through the clouds.

Seized with admiration, Li Yuan stood up, thinking that this spectacle was a sign from the god of the West. The calm immediately returned, and the young man heard the voice of the dragon.

"Before letting you pass to the opposite bank, I must know where you come from and where you are going! Know that I guard the entrance to the Country of the West, which is difficult to reach, and from which one does not always return."

"I come from the shores of Lake Tienn where my mother, who is old and miserable, is waiting for me. I am going to the Heaven of the West to meet the god of the West, for I have to ask him two questions for my mother and for myself!" answered Li Yuan, whose voice did not tremble.

"Can you tell me what these two questions are?" asked the dragon.

"I must know why the water of Lake Tienn is always dark, even when the sky is clear, and why I have to work every day of my life and still remain as poor as ever!" Li Yuan answered once again.

"Li Yuan, may luck be with you!" the dragon cried out to him. "I will take you across the river. But will you ask the god of the West something for me, too? For although I am a powerful dragon, I do not know the answer to this question."

"I will ask it," answered Li Yuan. "What do you wish to know?"

"I have lived in this river for over a thousand years," replied the dragon, "and in all that time I have never harmed a soul. I want to know why I have not received the power to fly in the air like all the other dragons of China."

"I promise you that I will ask the god of the West about that," said Li Yuan.

With this, the dragon came up to the river bank and told the boy to climb onto the large green scales of his back. Then the dragon, swimming carefully, brought him to the opposite bank of the river.

Li Yuan walked westward for another forty-eight days. On the evening of the forty-ninth day, he suddenly found himself in front of the entrance to a very large pagoda. Its roof was covered with jade and the door was guarded by two immense golden dragons. It was the pagoda of the god of the West. Li Yuan had arrived at the end of his journey!

From that moment on it seemed to Li Yuan that nothing bad could happen to him, and all his fatigue fell away. He demanded that the guards of the pagoda take him to the god of the West.

The young man followed the guards before whom great doors swung open by themselves, allowing them to pass through. Finally Li Yuan entered a sumptuous room with walls covered in gold. On a throne in the center of this grand room sat an old man with hair white as snow. At last Li Yuan stood face to face with the powerful god of the West!

"I know that you have come from far away to question me, and that in order to meet me you have endured all the hardships of a long voyage," said the god, addressing himself to Li Yuan. "But I must warn you that you are permitted to ask me only three questions! If by misfortune you ask me a fourth, you will not be able to obtain a single response from the god of the West, and all your effort will indeed have been in vain! If you have more than three questions to ask me, think, therefore, of the ones you can eliminate."

Li Yuan was at a loss. He could not make the god of the West wait any longer, and he felt that the two questions for which he had undertaken the trip were very important. But the three questions that were given to him by those who had helped him on his way made five. It was necessary then to put two aside.

The boy very quickly decided that to forget about himself in favor of the others was surely better and wiser than to think only of himself. He would ask the three questions that had been given to him and would not speak of his own.

The god of the West smiled, and he invited the young man to speak.

"The woman who gave me food and drink forty-eight days after I left Lake Tienn would like to know why her daughter, who is as beautiful as she is intelligent, has never spoken."

"Tell her that her daughter will speak the day a young man pleases her," answered the god.

Li Yuan bowed very low, touching his forehead to the ground, to show the god that he had understood very well and would bring the answer back to the woman. Then he went on to the second question.

"The old man who offered me his hospitality after I had been journeying another forty-eight days would like to know why the orange trees that he planted and has taken care of for fifty years have never given any fruit."

"Tell him on behalf of the god of the West, to first empty his cistern, then to dig deeply on that spot. He will take from the ground nine basins filled with gold and nine basins filled with silver. Then new water will spring up. When he sprinkles his orange trees with this water, they will blossom immediately and will soon give fruit—more than he could ever hope for."

Once again Li Yuan bowed to the ground to show the god of the West that he had understood very well and would bring back the answer to the old man.

Now there remained only the dragon's question. Completely forgetting his own questions, Li Yuan said, "The dragon who carried me across the river on his back and who guards the entrance to the Country of the West would like to know why he is condemned to swim for more than a thousand years in that tumultuous river while the other Chinese dragons can fly."

"Tell him on behalf of the god of the West to do two good deeds, for he has not done any in a thousand years. After that he will be able to fly like all the other Chinese dragons."

Very happy with the answers he was going to bring back, Li Yuan started on the return journey after once again bowing very low before the god of the West. He was anxious to see his mother, whom he had not forgotten for a single day in the course of his long journey.

From the edge of the river, Li Yuan saw shining in the distance the green scales of the dragon, who called to him.

"Young man, luck was with you, for you have seen the god of the West. Did you ask him my question?"

"The god of the West has charged me to tell you," answered Li Yuan, "to do two good deeds. After that you, too, will be able to fly through the air like all the Chinese dragons!"

"But what good deeds? For one hundred years I have scarcely seen a living soul pass by," thundered the dragon, whose green scales rose in anger.

"You could take me across the river again, for example," proposed the young man.

"That's exactly what I am going to do," answered the dragon, "and if you wish to accept it, I could also give you the green pearl that I have been wearing on my forehead for a thousand years!"

And he immediately carried Li Yuan on his green scales to the opposite bank of the river. Having arrived there, he pulled out from his forehead the pearl that shone in the night, and gave it to Li Yuan. Then with astonishment the boy saw the dragon immediately lift himself into the air.

"Thank you, Li Yuan! Keep my green pearl all your life!" he cried out, disappearing into the sky.

Since he had the pearl with him, it seemed to Li Yuan that the journey was much easier. He arrived very quickly at the home of the old man, who was waiting for him at the doorstep of his house.

"Young man, have you truly seen the god of the West? And did you ask him my question?"

"The god of the West has told me to tell you," answered Li Yuan, "to dig under your cistern. You will find there nine basins filled with gold and nine basins filled with silver. When you have taken them out, a spring of clear water will gush out of the bottom of your cistern. Then water your orange trees. They will become covered with blossoms, and soon their branches will bend under the weight of the fruit!"

The old man was too old to dig so deeply into the ground, so Li Yuan offered to help him. He had to dig a long time to get to the bottom of the cistern, which first he had to empty of all its water. As soon as the basins were taken out of the ground, clear water sprang up from the bottom of the cistern, which then became a wonderful well. Dazzled, the old man and the

young one watched the orange trees become covered with flowers as soon as they received a little water from this well.

Li Yuan stayed several days with the old man, never tiring of admiring the orange trees, which were already covered with fruit. Then he wished to start on his journey again, but the old man did not let him leave empty-handed.

"Now that I am old, my marvelous well and my orange trees are enough to make me happy for the rest of my life," said the old man to Li Yuan. "Take with you, therefore, all the gold and silver that you dug out of the ground for me. You did not ask the god of the West anything for yourself. At least you will have these riches!"

With much emotion, Li Yuan left the old man and, carrying the green pearl of the dragon and all the gold and silver the old man had given him in gratitude, he started out once again on his journey.

The young man soon arrived at the home of the woman whose daughter was mute. The woman rushed to meet him and asked him, "Young man, have you really seen the god of the West? And did you ask him my question?"

"The god of the West has this to tell you—your daughter will speak the day a young man pleases her!"

At this moment, the young girl, whose name meant Morning Dew, entered the room.

She was astonished and confused to find there a strange young man of whom her mother had never spoken. She found him very handsome. Her beautiful face lit up with emotion, and smilingly she asked her mother, "Mother, who is this young man?"

The mother cried with happiness, and answered her daughter. "He is Li Yuan, the one you are to marry, for the god of the West has predicted that when you meet a young man who pleases you, speech will be given to you at last! You have spoken today for the first time—let this day be your wedding day!"

And it was thus that Li Yuan married the lovely Morning Dew whom he loved from the moment he met her.

The young groom was anxious to get back to his mother, who had been waiting for him for so long. But he was still sad because he was not bringing back the answers to his own two questions.

He had brought home a most beautiful bride, but his poor mother's eyes had become so worn out that she could not see her new daughter-in-law. However the old woman passed her hands over the lovely face of Morning Dew and smiled kindly at her.

And Li Yuan had come home laden with gold and silver. He made the coins jingle so his mother could hear them and rejoice with him over these new riches.

Finally, he wanted his mother to admire the wonderful green pearl — the gift of the dragon. Its light was dazzling, but the worn-out eyes of the old woman no longer saw anything but the dark night.

Li Yuan exclaimed, still holding the green pearl in his hand, "Ah, green pearl, how happy I would be now if only our mother could see!"

And at that very moment old Li Hao's sight was restored to her!

Immediately Li Yuan understood that the green pearl of the dragon was magic since it made his wish come true. Then all three of them left the little house and walked towards Lake Tienn.

Li Yuan exclaimed, "Green pearl, make the water of our lake become blue as the sky!"

At once the dark water of the lake became blue and transparent just as Li Yuan wished.

From that moment on, Li Yuan did not have to beg his pearl for anything very often because happiness reigned under his roof. He worked joyfully and his life became as sweet as honey on the shores of Lake Tienn, which was forever blue.